# Climbing Back

Gilly Mara

# DEDICATION

There are many I wish to dedicate this to who feature in this book; from my current work colleagues who have been really supportive to all those in the paddling community. From my long suffering family who have watched me go out and pursue my goals, missing many family functions to achieve them. To my friends who come and share my adventures with me and make me smile when the going gets tough. Kim and Jen you taught me to laugh and talk when I didn't want to. Sam I owe my life to you and I am forever in your debt, you a very special, selfless and giving person. To Paul who has been my friend and mentor for many years and given me that kick to make a plan when I feel lost; to Carl who has been my backstop and provided me the solid ground for me to grow and achieve my paddling dreams; to my physio and friend Gill Gillespie who has put me back together both physically and mentally on many occasions. Then finally to Tessa Lukehurst, who I told my story to and who helped put all of my jumbled words and sections of my life together and helped me for the first time find calm from my mountain adventure. I truly could not have turned my ramblings I first wrote three months after my accident into what it looks like now.

My wish is for you to read this and be inspired, to look upon a barrier as a challenge, as a challenge can be overcome even when it seems impossible. The first step or stroke is the hardest, but I promise you it gets easier, you can do it. I have found you have more people behind you than you can actually imagine :o).

# CONTENTS

# ACKNOWLEDGMENTS

Tessa Lukehurst whom this book was told to and Clifford Vince who created the cover image.

# 1 FALLING

Sixty feet seems a long way when you're looking up at it. It looks even further when it's below you, you're perched on an outcrop without a rope and your foot is beginning to slip.

"I can't hold on much longer," I shouted to Mike, on the other side of the rock.

"Yes, you can," he replied. "You have to."

He couldn't see the situation the way I could. Everything we had done led us inexorably to this point. My right hand was scrabbling for grip in a crack in the rock. My left hand was slipping with sweat on a root and my right foot was in the air. Going back wasn't an option; the root was my only way back and it was pulling out of the rock. It was as if I had known I was going to fall all day. Going forwards was beyond my reach. I just wasn't as tall as Mike and there were no holds for me. There was only one direction left but I knew I had given in.

We were walking on the Sandia Mountain near Albuquerque in New Mexico. For Mike and I, at the end of a long summer working, the plan had been to walk up the La Luz Trail to watch the sunset before running back on an easier route. We were young and fit and we had expected a pleasant walk up to the 12,000 foot peak but everything had gone wrong. Our friendship, based on a belief that we were soul mates, was breaking down. Distracted, we had strayed from the trail and were working our way back towards it when we found ourselves committed to rounding this craggy outcrop to get down.

I only needed to bring my right leg round the rock face to be safe. It just wasn't long enough and the harder I tried the more I was beginning to slide from my precarious perch. I tried to bring my right foot back and place it on top of my left, but I couldn't get a grip. My body was getting heavier by the second and I could already feel myself falling.

My thoughts began to slow down. My mind had been racing, to find a solution to the situation I was in, trying to work out what options I had and which might give the best result. I became blasé. I knew now that falling was inevitable and I began to accept it. My heart beat slowed down to a more regular pattern and no longer felt like it was going to jump out from my chest, my breathing stopped being shallow. I had accepted and was about to embrace my fate.

"Push up with your legs!" Mike called. I tried to push on my left leg and took a deep breath.

"No, no, I can't. I'm sorry," I told him. I really couldn't, but suddenly the panic was gone. My hands seemed to have a will of their own as they released.

"I'm sorry," I called again, apologising both to Mike and to myself. I instinctively pushed away with my feet and my mind went clear. My body felt quite loose and free as I fell. I had no fear and I was quite relaxed. Somehow I was certain that I would be alright. The thought that I might die didn't enter my head for so much as a second. I was at peace for the first time in hours and time was irrelevant. I just let my body do what it needed to do.

For me, my impact was a silent movie. It could have been happening to someone else. My right hip struck first and I rolled across my back making a diagonal and then I was flying again. It was almost like performing back flips on a trampoline. Time was running slowly and it felt as if I was flying forever before I hit the ground, rolling from my hips, my head leaving the ground last, my body light once again. I was high on the sensation; I was on a rollercoaster leaving my stomach behind as I rose. I almost wanted to shout "Wheee" as I bounced again and again. There was nothing I could do to stop it. I was rolling, tumbling and out of control.

My brain caught up with me after about five hits. The time had come to try to stop myself. I flung my arms out as if to catch hold of something, but there was nothing to hold. I bounced into the air for the sixth time and tried again. This time I slowed the rotation a little so I tried to extend my legs as well. I hit the ground with the left side of my body and my right arm and leg thumped into the ground. My body tried to roll again but it just didn't have enough momentum. There was no sound, no colour, no thought and no pain. For a few moments the world and I just paused together.

As my senses returned I began the audit of my body. I ran my tongue over my teeth. They were all there. I checked them individually and none were broken. My toes were next. I was pleased to find that I could wiggle them. Fingers? They were fine; right hand, then left. After that my knees and elbows twitched. I seemed to be in one piece and nothing was hurting. I couldn't see though, so I tried to call out and then I knew that I was in trouble after all. I could hear myself in my head, calling "Hello" but I knew that there was no sound. It was as if I had laryngitis. I tried again, calling to Mike:

"Hello...hello...I'm here, hello," but there was nothing.

"Gilly! Gilly! Are you ok? Talk to me!" Mike's voice was a welcome sound. "Speak to me, Gilly! Are you ok?" The panic in his voice was clear, he was trying to find me and I just wanted to relax his fear and say I'm fine, don't worry.

I still had no voice and no vision. I tried again and chuckled to myself. I've always found it funny when I lose my voice and live in a world where I am the only one who can hear me. I repeated hello, going from a low to a high pitch and eventually a little squeak came out.

"Hello?"

I moved my right hand towards my face and began to check my head. I had opened my eyes but the world hadn't come back. It was a deep monotonous shade of black. I continued to feel my body. It was slightly curled up, leaning to the left and my legs were lower than my head. I could hear Mike now, calling and coming closer. There was still no pain, but I knew things weren't right. I don't panic easily. In intense situations I try to amuse myself to relax. It helps me gain control and organise what I need to do.

"Hello, I'm here! I guess this blows Poland, doesn't it?" I had been looking forward to competing in the Student World Championships, what would be my first international in two weeks and although I didn't know how badly I was hurt, I knew I wouldn't be able to compete. I moved my hand over my left eye towards my hairline and felt sticky blood, then something smooth and hard in the middle. As I probed it with my fingers I realised that it was my skull.

At that moment, the rustle of Mike's footsteps came close and I paused with my fingers perched on the top of my head. He took my hand from my head.

"You've cut your head," he told me. My sight was coming slowly back and I could see his face. He was very pale as he examined me. It is an image I will never forget; it said so many things without him saying a word. Suddenly I was scared to. His shocked expression told the story of how I looked, his reactions showed the extent of my damage. In that instant I knew that this was serious and if I wanted to survive I would have to take control. I broke eye contact and tried to look somewhere else. My memory has blocked his face from this point. I remember his eyes, but I have no memory of his face. I couldn't let his fear infect me.

My arms were relatively undamaged, so I moved on to checking my legs. I tried to prop myself up to make it easier and the first jolt of pain shocked through my right leg. Perhaps it was broken? My eyes were looking down at my leg, but yet I couldn't see it. I asked Mike to check and he ran his hands over it. He couldn't feel anything out of place which reassured me because I felt as if I had bone sticking out near my hip. I tried to focus on the relief that he had brought me and ignore the messages that moving had started to send to my brain.

My left shin was cut to the bone. I was caught up in amazement at the whiteness of the exposed tibia before Mike took off his T-shirt and started to bind it up. He took my tank top out of the rucksack and put it over my head.

"We have to get you off this hill," his voice was shaking. "We have to get you out of here."

As an outdoor sports coach I had been through hours of first aid training. I knew that after a fall I had potential spinal injuries and shouldn't move. But the panic was rising in his tone of voice. It communicated itself to me and my training went out of the window. I wanted to get off the mountain with him, all logic gone.

He took hold of my right hand and pulled me into a more upright position. I held myself up with my hands flat on either side of me and looked around, taking stock. My legs were almost straight out in front, my right knee higher than my left. The colours were fading back into the world and I was fascinated by the details of my surroundings. My heart was racing now, the world was trying to catch up from its earlier pause and I could feel a cool wind behind me. In front of me was the peak of the mountain where we should have been standing as the sun began to set. The greens and browns of the cacti around me were merging. The orange and pink of the sand and rocks were turning red as time ran out on the day.

Mike knelt in front of me, still holding my right arm.

"I don't care how long it takes, even if you have to shuffle your way out. I want to hear all your whines of pain." His voice was desperate and shaky. He got up and left me for a moment, disappearing behind a bush.

I wanted to get off the mountain. I tried to move myself forward. I pushed down with my hands to lift my bottom up and swing myself up. I moved my left foot forward and stopped as the pain in my hips intensified. I tried again, but it was no use. My body, that had been silent for so long, was screaming at me not to move. I had moved less than a centimetre and I now knew that there was something very wrong. I called Mike back.

"I'm staying here, there's no way I can move. You are going to have to go down and get help."

"I'm not leaving you here," he told me, firmly. "You can do it. We'll do this together. Tell me where it's hurting. You can do it." He was pleading with me, his desperation with the situation very apparent.

He took hold of my hand once more and began tugging at me, desperately trying to help me move my tired body, but it just set fireworks off in my body. Much as I wanted to be down and off the mountain I knew it wouldn't work. I took stock of the situation and knew there was only one option that would give me a chance of getting off the mountain alive.

"I can't. I'm not able to go." I forced myself to speak with the calm that I needed to stay in control, even though inside I was a quivering wreck. "You're going to have to go down and get help." He got onto his knees.

"I can't leave you."

"You have to. I really can't move."

I took quite a while to convince him that it was the right thing to do. He really didn't want to leave me, but he thought it was only my leg that was the problem. I couldn't bring myself to tell him that it was a lot worse. I knew that my hips were badly hurt and I was becoming sure that there was something wrong with my neck. He was in complete shock and I didn't want to add to his problems. Eventually he calmed down and I persuaded him to go for help. I gave him my wallet with contact phone numbers and reminded him to call 911 because this was the States and not the UK. We shared out the water and he made me as comfortable as he could before going.

As Mike left he gave me a kiss on the head. It was a symbol of hope for both of us and we both needed it badly. We shouted to each other as he descended and as he disappeared into the distance I hoped I would see him again, and soon. I could hear his voice fading away and kept calling back to him until I was alone in the desert evening.

# 2 THE LONG DARKNESS

We don't often experience silence in this modern world. Despite the Sandia Mountain's proximity to the city of Albuquerque I could only hear my breathing and my heart. In restful moments in the past I have often concentrated on them, counting beats and breaths, but now I couldn't concentrate. I sat watching and staring where I had last seen Mike and time flicked past me. Without realising, the world around me had begun to go into its sleepy night phase. My current sitting position needed to be changed, to try and protect myself from the cold and rising pain. I felt exposed and alone, I wriggled around, trying to find a comfortable position. I lowered myself until I was on my left side, right leg on top of left, in a foetal position. My head lay on something I couldn't see, but it felt like a rock. On my right, a backpack, and by my right hand our last bottle of water. My right leg was aching but in the late evening heat I wasn't in any pain yet. I resolved to lie very still and to avoid moving again. I slowly began to relax. I could think clearly. This was the first time I had been alone all summer and I tried to make the most of it. I wanted to think freely, to find insights or reflect, but I couldn't.

For a long time I focussed on the spot where I had last seen Mike. In the riot of red rocks, brown soils and melon greens that spot was somehow more vibrant. . It was the focus of my hope; the last place I had seen anyone living and, perhaps, the place where rescue would reappear. Above and around me my field of view was restricted by my immobility. There was a ridge line in front of me and the top of the mountain a little behind, but I couldn't see it properly. I would have to move for that. I stared at it all, trying to assemble the sizes and shapes of the rocks it was made of.

I had no immediate sense of fear. I knew that I was badly hurt and yet I seemed to be detached from the seriousness of my situation. I believe survival in difficult situations comes down to a lot of factors; luck (I needed a fair amount of that), mental toughness (how long and deep could I dig into my mind to keep myself going, was unknown and frightened me), fitness (I was confident of that), determination.

The day's climbing seemed a long way away from me now. The sun was setting and the desert warmth was receding. I made the most of the sunset. One of our objectives when we planned our day had been to watch the sun set before we left. The sun had been missing for most of the day, but for a brief moment it returned, bringing me an unexpected gift. It was beautiful and another brief distraction. I could see two tiny Tram cars descending on the cable that ran to the top of the mountain and felt happy for the passengers, that they had such a marvellous sight to enjoy. As the sun went down the heat left my body and was replaced by an ever increasing pain.

The air felt cool and refreshing. My lips were dry and chapped. The makeshift bandage on my head began to come loose. At first it didn't bother me but as the wind increased it plucked at the ends, creating a vibration that began to annoy me. Like someone tapping their foot or hand on something, you can tolerate it for a moment and then you just snap. I decided that I had to tighten it. It was easier thought than done. My right arm wouldn't respond and it took all of my concentration to move it. My coordination had gone and natural movement was beyond me. It took separate thoughts and instructions to my hand and then my elbow to move them towards my head. Gravity had helped me to lower myself earlier, but now it was definitely working against me. When I finally persuaded my arm to move my hand brushed past my hair and I realised that the hat I had worn to protect me from the desert sun had gone. Previously tied in a pony tail, my hair was tangled into a large knot, held in place with twigs and leaves.

I forgot the bandage. My hair distracted me and seemed to be a bigger problem. I was worried if I couldn't get the twigs out they would have to cut my hair, or worse shave it all off. My long hair was part of my identity. If they took that away, I wouldn't be me; people might not recognise me. The pain, where I was, my difficulties were shelved, the only thing that mattered at that point in time was my hair. So I tried to fix it, pulling the sticks away and teasing at the knots. It was all too much effort. I was flattened and almost let my inner emotions come forward, but then a trigger of "If you let that happen you might not survive" came back to me. I felt a tear run down my face. I had spent my summer full of the kind of energy that permits you to run before a busy day canoeing and bounce everywhere. Now the weight of my arm was too much for me to hold it by my head. I let it fall, resting until I had the energy to move it back to my side. My senses came back to me and I evaluated my previous thought. Of all the things to worry about, my hair, I smiled. I reflected that if my University friends could have seen me panicking about my hair, they would wonder what had come over me. I thought of Sally and Sharon. I could hear their northern accents in my head and a little warmth came over me. Another tear trickled over my cheek and slowly dripped into the dirt. I wished one of them could be with me, for comfort.

I lost all track of time. A cooling breeze picked up as the sun went below the ridge, the silence replaced by a rustle of leaves in the bushes around me. It never seemed to get completely dark. The vibrant desert colours faded slowly after the sun went down. The plants and rocks around me became outlines, silhouettes of shadows with soft edges. The Tram cars became tiny square boxes of light that sometimes seemed to pause and flash at me. When they stopped I knew it was ten o'clock. It was the only occasion on which I knew what the time was in the whole night.

The Trams stopping brought home to me that I was alone and injured on this mountain. I wished I had been on one of those Tram cars. My nose was running from the cold and all I could do was twitch my lips when it itched. Even that small movement felt wrong as my face tightened with crusted blood. I began to feel sorry for myself. Everything ached and I was cold. In the heat of an Albuquerque morning setting off for our adventure in a one piece bathing suit, with shorts and a T-shirt for warmth hadn't seemed like a poor decision. I wasn't so sure now. I closed my eyes in the vain hope that when I opened them again it would all have been a nightmare and Mum would be there to hug me better. Then it struck me. My only real hope was that Mike had got down off the mountain and raised the alarm. What if he hadn't? What if he came across another drop, one he didn't dare climb?

I could feel panic rising within me and knew that it really wouldn't do. If I was going to survive this I needed to stay calm and stay awake. I decided to sing. A silly tune has to be the best way there is to cheer yourself up. 'The Sound of Music' has always been one of my favourite films. I love the way Maria sings about her favourite things to cheer herself up and I had borrowed this idea and sung about my troubles before. Nothing came easily to mind so I began to invent a tune and sang about lying on the side of a mountain hoping someone would come. Having just spent the summer at camp in Pennsylvania it was campfire tunes and rounds that came to mind. The chorus and some of the versus, went something along the lines of;

"I've cut my head and blood is running down my face
It's making my face feel crusty
My leg is cut and I can see the bone
The skin around it's becoming tighter
I'm pretty sure I've broken something
As the pain is like nothing I've ever had before

[CHORUS] So, here I am, stuck on the mountain,
I'm lying on my side,
Please can you come and help me
Cos I'm not sure what else I can do.
Can anyone out there hear me sing?
If not I had best shout a little louder...

I'm getting scared now; the pain is making me shake
Tears are forming in my eyes
I can't seem to stop thinking about my fate
I know I need to be positive
But I have lost all my happy thoughts
My mind is consumed with all bad things. So..."
[CHORUS – sung/shouted a little louder]

I sang louder and louder in the vain hope that someone would hear me but it didn't really work. I began to cry and, as the song grew louder, so did my sobs until they choked out the song. My morale was at its lowest so far.

I stopped and gave in for a while, but I knew that it was a luxury I couldn't afford. If getting through things is all about your attitude of mind, you have to develop the capability to train your attitude. What I needed was a tune that would make me laugh, so I switched to the Hokey

Cokey'. It worked. It was still hard, but my mood was improving. I went through 'The whole repertoire we had used at Camp Weequahic and then repeated it, adding humorous ripostes that described my situation. It worked. As I sang I became convinced that I could hear someone responding to me. I lay still, quieting my breath and listening as hard I could. There was nothing. I called out and heard it again. There was someone else out there! I shouted as loud as I could and this time I could hear it clearly. It was an echo. Instead of depressing me it made me laugh. I couldn't have asked for a better distraction. I ran the gamut of echo noises, from Cooee to Yodelayhee. Each time the echo went on for ages and I tried as hard as I could to get the echoes to last for longer each time. It was like being in a big theatre with amazing acoustics and I explored them to the best of my ability. It wasn't until sometime later that I learned that the ravine into which we had strayed was known as Upper Echo Canyon. It was well named. There were stars above me and they were my audience, but I didn't really need one. It's fortunate for me that I can so easily entertain myself.

Eventually I switched back to singing. I began with ten green bottles, but it was too short. I didn't like the quiet. It felt unnatural. I started with an American version that we'd been singing at camp, but decided it was wrong. I switched to the English version so that if any rescuers heard me they would know that I was the lost English girl. One chorus was too short so I started again from one thousand. I set myself targets. I challenged myself with each hundred green bottles in the hope that rescue would arrive. I began crying as I sang, again. I was losing track and repeating myself. Somewhere around nine hundred and something I lost track of time and everything else.

Time must have flown past. The stars had gone and it was spitting with rain. I knew I hadn't been asleep. Sleep just doesn't feel like that; I must have blacked out. It scared me. I had to stay conscious and awake. There was a chance that if I let go again I might not wake up. I really didn't want that. My situation was serious. Physically there was nothing I could do. I knew I was too badly hurt to move. I had no idea how long I had been up there. I didn't have a watch; that was both good and bad. Knowing the time might have told me whether I could reasonably expect to be rescued and yet there was a good chance that I might become fixated by time passing.

Rain is rare in this area. It seldom rains for long or very hard and it is usually welcomed for bringing life to what would otherwise be an arid and terrifying landscape. Today, for a change, the life giving rain intensified, falling in showers, passing over me on a cool breeze. It brought new smells with it; the welcome aroma of parched soil absorbing moisture after a drought was comforting at first, but as the rain grew stronger the smell changed and made me feel dirty. I began to shiver as the damp worked its way through my inadequate swimsuit. The shivering from the cold and the shaking from the pain consumed my mind and it took everything I could muster to concentrate on controlling each muscle in turn to stop it. I became a sergeant major, commanding the muscles and congratulating myself out loud whenever I succeeded. It was short term; it took too much energy from me. It was also focusing on the things that were wrong. I needed something different so I went back to the green bottles, starting at around seven hundred and fifty to allow for lost time.

When you have lots of things to do time seems to fly past. Waiting for rescue on a mountain slows it down. The rain grew gradually heavier and more constant. It slowly drew the heat out of my body. I remembered that Mike had put his t-shirt over my left leg to stop the bleeding before he left. I reached slowly for it and found that it had almost fallen off. I carefully pulled it up and dragged it over my head, putting my right arm through the sleeve first. By carefully tugging the material over and past my left shoulder I was able to cover most of my upper body. I rested for a while as the extra layer provided some of the warmth I was desperate for. The t-shirt smelt of Mike and for a moment I took comfort in feeling close to someone I knew. I fantasised that he was right next to me, and the predicament I was in was actually some strange adventure; this was just one of many challenges someone had set for us to overcome.

The rain quickly washed the fantasy away; my uncovered left arm was numb with cold. I made another attempt to pull the t-shirt under my upper arm and down the side of my torso. I kept tugging at it with my good arm until I was able to stretch it down past my hip. I pulled my knees up until they were covered by the t-shirt. Eventually I moved my right arm out of the sleeve and put it inside. None of the small gains in warmth lasted long. I had stopped singing and didn't want to start again; the words were becoming jumbled; I couldn't remember the numbers and it was frightening me.

I focussed all my effort into breathing to try to control my shivering. The shaking felt as if I was a steam train going up and down hills. The downhill sections were frantic and out of control, then I would manage to restore decorum, slow my heart rate down, and almost feel like I was in control of the shaking. For a few moments there was relief: it had stopped and I took the opportunity to enjoy breathing in and out again, then I would be over the top of another hill and all I could do was try to keep control for as long as I could. It became a never ending game, up and down, up and down. The down sections went on for longer and longer. I longed for a flat section, but never got one. The exhaustion took hold of me and I drifted into a deathly sleep.

When I next opened my eyes I was really thankful not to be shaking. Time had once more passed. I tried to make sense of my surroundings. I could see two ridges above me. One was the top of the mountain. I could see where the Tram lines finished near the peak. There was another ridge and between them they framed my view of the sky. All around me I could see the silhouettes of plants. They were probably cacti. If I had felt able to move my arm I might have touched one. All week they had been attracting me in their lovely shades of melon, but now that small movement was too much to contemplate. I wriggled and slowly manoeuvred myself a few degrees anticlockwise, fighting the pain, trying to see where I had come from; the rock face that I had fallen from. It was in vain, everything was too dark and the new position was much less comfortable. Worse, it had a much more restricted view. I slowly wriggled back to where I had been and lay still, exhausted by this small effort.

For a long time I didn't even have the energy to raise my eyes from the bush in front of me. Eventually I did and there, on the nearer of the two ridges was a light. A thrill ran through me. My imagination ran off with possible explanations. My rational mind quickly dismissed a spiritual explanation, which left me with a rescue party. It hung where I had first seen it for a while, then it seemed to move closer, growing bigger as it came towards me. There was no way that rescuers could approach me in that manner or at that speed. The nearer it came the bigger it grew. I wanted to lift my arm and touch it, but my fingers just twitched in the dirt. The light had a calming and warming influence on me. I managed to lift my right arm, but no matter how hard I tried I couldn't grip it. I couldn't grip it with my mind either. The light was surreal. It engrossed me, it warmed me and I embraced it. For a while there was nothing but the light; it took away the pain, my immobility and my shivers. My whole body felt free and weightless and I began gravitating towards the light, I was being taken away from the mountainside and my battered body. The light was smiling at me and in return I couldn't help but smile back at it. I was engrossed and intrigued with the light. It made me feel strong and stand tall and it was as if my feet had a mind of their own and were swinging as if I was taking footsteps but I was above the ground. I don't know why, but I hesitated, my legs stopped swinging. I looked over my right shoulder away from the light and saw my own body curled up in a ball in the darkness below me. It made me stop smiling and sadness came upon me. The body looked fragile and lifeless all on its own. I was intrigued by the fact there were no other describable features around it. I could only see my body. I turned around and took one step towards it, to see if I could make out any features. As I did so I looked over my left shoulder, back towards the light, and heard someone speaking deep within me. I couldn't quite make out the words. I wasn't sure what to do and just stood there, the light to my left side and the body to my right. I felt as if I had to make a decision. I had been ready to give up on life, to go wherever this amazing light took me. I glanced down at the body and in that moment I decided "Not Now. Not yet" And I went back.

It felt as if there was a warm breeze behind me. It comforted me like the breath of someone who loved me, holding me and caressing me, pinning me back in the world. I had so many things still to do and achieve. I saw images of my friends: university friends; paddling friends; my family: mum, dad, my big sister Claire and my younger brother Josh; I remembered all the places I wanted to visit: the Grand Canyon; the Great Wall of China; Japan; Central Park in New York: all the goals I wanted to achieve: representing my country and completing my degree. They were rushing through my mind like a tornado. Each word or image was picked up and tossed about until they became a mangled blur. When I tried to look back the light had gone. I was in tears. On the one hand I felt an intense shame that I had been so close to giving up, but on the other I felt an intense grief for it. I wanted to feel the warmth, the release that it had brought. I wanted it to take me away from this hillside and the pain that was beginning to rise from my very bones. I knew I had done the right thing. That voice was like a parent, someone who loved me, reminding me that I still had something to achieve. I wish I knew what it was.

A little later I was sure I heard voices passing close to me. I was paranoid, unsure if they were people, angels or devils. I no longer had any idea what was real. I kept quiet and they passed me by. I was worried that I was losing contact with reality and would never get down from this mountain. I only knew that I had to. I had an opportunity; to improve myself, to be less selfish, to achieve more and to get it right. I wanted that second chance at my life.

# 3 WAITING FOR RESCUE

It wasn't obvious to me while I was alone on the mountain, but there was a lot happening down below. We were staying with my friend Sam and she takes up the story of getting a rescue out.

When I dropped Gilly and Mike at the foot of the Sandia Tram Line on Thursday morning I was already worried. I thought the itinerary they had chosen was ambitious and that they weren't well prepared. Although American hiking trails are well marked, they had little experience hiking here in the desert. I wasn't sure they had enough water or were prepared for their walk at that high altitude. Despite having been out on their own a couple of days before, this time they planned a longer, more committing walk. Normally I would plan to do one trail in a day, but they intended to go up by the La Luz Trail and down by another.

Watching them walk away from my car I had a strange feeling that things would go wrong. Gilly's assurances that they were experienced, Mike's mountain leadership qualification and Gilly's fitness were all very well, but a summer leading in a pursuit centre in the Welsh Mountains or spent leading canoeing in Pennsylvania don't necessarily prepare you for high desert mountains.

Unlike my British friends I was already back at school and facing a punishing schedule. I had a double set of classes and a job to fit in with moving into a new apartment with my friends. Inviting Gilly to stay was something I had really wanted to do. She helped me out when I was struggling as a counsellor at Camp Weequahic, giving me advice and moving me into her cabin so that I didn't have to go home. She was a fun, wonderful person and when she expressed a desire to travel a little before going home I had no hesitation inviting her to visit me in Albuquerque.

All through that long day I struggled with a premonition that things had gone wrong. I wasn't surprised when I arrived at the designated collection point at the prearranged time of 7:30 to find it empty. I was already panicking, but I gave them another half an hour to turn up before I rang my Dad for advice. He did his best to keep me calm, but his advice was stark.

"You can ring Search and Rescue now, or we could just make sure they aren't in the wrong place first." He offered to come out and check the other car parks so that I could stay put. We were still discussing the best options when a car pulled in beside mine and I was terrified to see a very battered Mike get out. He looked as if he had been for a ride in a blender: his clothes were tattered and streaked with blood from encounters with desert vegetation and small falls on his headlong descent. His face was white and his eyes were staring with shock, but he had made it off the mountain and found some helpers. They had called the Rescue Services and brought him here to meet me. The State Police didn't take long to arrive and my dusty car park became the communications centre for the rescue attempt.

A very kind Officer let us listen in on their communications and it was clear that this was being treated as a very serious incident. If we had any doubts we only had to look at Mike as he pored over a map spread on the bonnet of a State Trooper's car, trying to identify the exact place of the fall. It wasn't easy, they had possibly never even been on the trail and there wasn't a lot to identify the place from. Before long there were two helicopters in the area, dropping search teams and hurrying to get the search started before it could get dark. It wasn't possible to take these helicopters right into the search area because they would be flying too close to the Tram lines, so teams were being dropped as close as possible.

We could hear yelling from the hillside and radio chatter as the search got under way but the light was already fading and so were my hopes. Before long the night had closed in and we were, shivering. I refused to go home, so my friend brought us blankets up from town and we waited, wrapped in them, wondering what we could possibly tell Gilly's parents. Listening in the conversations of the rescue teams on the radio we knew this was a serious situation. To hear from my parents, on the phone, that the search had made the TV News made it worse.

As the rescue helicopters ran low on fuel and search hours the State Police called the National Guard who supplied a smaller helicopter, equipped with night vision equipment and able to fly closer to the Tram wires. The search went on through the seemingly endless night. Rain made things worse and, on top of the injuries Gilly had to have sustained in her fall, we began to worry about hypothermia. In the middle of the night the radio brought the news that someone had heard her respond to a call. Our relief was indescribable. She was still alive and we began to believe that she would be brought down.

As the light grew in the early morning we could see the helicopter begin to circle, looking for the right place and then it reported that it was out of fuel and would have to return to base. I couldn't believe that we were so close to finding her and were going to lose our best hope of getting her off the mountain quickly. I began to badger them to stay as long as they possibly could and it made the difference we needed. Minutes later they found her. We were elated. There was a pause as they checked with control that it really was her, and not a search team. We shouted at the radio, almost drowning out the operators, that it was her, please pick her up. Then we heard them say that they would drop a winch man to recover her. Everything accelerated. They seemed to pluck her off the mountain in seconds and were flying back towards the city. The helicopter had insufficient fuel to take her straight to the hospital so they landed on the nearest road, the Tramway Boulevard, and transferred her to an ambulance. Mike and I followed it to the hospital.

Because my mum was an ER nurse I knew my way around a little and we were able to see Gilly in triage. Her white face contrasted bleakly with the blood from her head wound. She looked terrified and in real pain, but the first thing she said to me was: "I guess this means I won't be going to the International." It's typical of her spirit that she has to joke at a time like this. My pleasure at seeing her alive and joking was tempered by seeing her in a spinal brace. I was sure that she would be paralysed and that her active lifestyle was already over.

# 4 ALONE WITH THE SKY

High on the Sandia Mountain the pain had become the only constant in the never ending night. It was rising from my bones; intense and continuous; everywhere, from my toes to the roots of my hair. It's hard to find the words to describe it; the pain was wordless, colourless, all I could do was curl up and try to stop my body from tensing up completely. It had been hours and with every minute it seemed to get worse. I kept telling myself that it couldn't last forever. It was finite, therefore, it would stop eventually. The only end would be rescue. I was stubborn. There was no other option for ending the pain. I just had to hold on and wait until the pain became more bearable.

I was curled up into the tightest ball I could get myself into, my arms drawn into my t-shirt and wrapped around my knees but I was still wet through. I had been in this position for a long time and was getting fidgety. I was fighting against the cold, the pain, it was a never ending fight and one I was becoming ever more tired of, I had to keep digging deeper into my mind to keep my emotions together and stay positive.

The pain had got into my soul and the hours of it had

slowly destroyed all of the happy and safe places I had safely stored into my memories. I had used them to take me away from the pain. Ones I had consciously or subconsciously drawn upon to get me through tough times in the past, either when feeling sad, unwell, lonely, or as inspiration to let me know I could achieve something. I would stare out and go into a dreamlike state and take myself back to a happy memory. Now though, in my present state, I could not recollect the feel of the water on my finger tips, whilst I floated along with my feet on the deck of my plastic boat with the sun shining on my legs and face. I wanted to bring back the adrenaline rush, exhilaration and sense of achievement I got from paddling a speed run down the River Etive in Scotland, just a few months before, in February. I tried to remember the safe feeling of stroking the family dog, Sally. I tried stroking the side of my face to rekindle that thought, but it too provided little comfort and could not take the pain away. My last and sacred memory was all I had left: to be wrapped and held by my Mum, with my head on her chest, her arms wrapped around me and me curled around her, like I was a small child. It was my last safe place: a final refuge to try to take my mind away from the pain.

I was in a never ending nightmare. As a child my Mum would say to me: 'Try lying in a new position to see if that would stop your bad dream', it never failed to work and I was able to sleep. I was longing for the pain to stop and to sleep. I tried to turn myself over and lie on my back. I had to lift each limb one at a time, moving slowly and carefully to avoid making any damage worse. As I finally rolled over onto my back it felt as someone had placed a rock under my skin. I moved my right hand in underneath my lower back and found a lump that felt as if it was the size of a rugby ball. It made my face scrunch up and my eyes squint with the pain and draw in a shallow breath, but moving into this position had taken all of my energy. I couldn't move straight back over onto my side. I had to lie there in additional pain for a while as I gathered the strength to move again, my nightmare hadn't got better it had just got worse.

I took a deep breath and began, moving single limbs again, my inner sergeant major barking the commands. As I rolled back towards my side I ran out of strength and had to give up midway. I managed to manoeuvre a rock below my head to support it. At least it had eased the pain a little. My motivation finally began to dwindle. I tried to close my eyes and put myself into a happier place, but I could no longer dream one up. I had no happy thoughts left and began to lose hope. The pain had reached and destroyed my last sacred place. I wanted to kick and scream, to tell the world I was still here; to have a giant toddler's paddy and scream my frustration with what was happening to me. I had no energy, no movement. I couldn't even scream. I instinctively, lifted a hand to my face and stroked it gently, trying to recapture the comfort that my Mother had given me when I was young, but to no avail.

I had been on the verge of so much potential in my life. For the first time, at the end of that summer I had everything lined up. I was going to be an International Canoeist; I knew what I wanted to do with my working life when I finished my degree; my American adventure had freed me from the constraints of my childhood and in a single day all of that and more was slipping from my fingers. It was gone and if I closed my eyes now the rest would follow it. I might never taste, touch or smell anything more. I might leave my body behind on this dirty mountainside and I had no idea of where I might then be. I fiercely fought against losing hold with everything I had. I lost the battle.

When I woke up the sky had changed again. There were shades of blue lightening it and I had stopped shivering. Where was this place, where had the pain gone? I tried to recall my conversations with echoes in the night and called out a gentle "Cooee".

"Hello," the echo replied.

My eyes shot open. If I could have sat up I would have been bolt upright.

"Hello," I called back, as loudly as I could. There was no response. I called again and again and then it came again.

"Hello." It was faint, definitely not an echo. My heart was pounding. Was I on Earth? Then everything came together, I was still alive, I finally knew that Mike had made it and help was coming. I just had to stay awake and keep alert. My finite time with pain was becoming a definable number. I called back, hoping we could have a conversation.

"Where. Are. You?" I split the simple question up into single words, hoping that the echo would carry it and we could have a conversation. There was an indistinct response so I reverted to "Hello" and yodelling. I heard another "Hello" back and then what seemed to be "We are on our way." They had to be a long way away but it didn't matter. They were on their way and that meant that they would find me.

At dawn the rain came back, with a vengeance. It also brought heavier gusts of wind. I listened out and as the rustling from the trees and bushes got louder I knew the next gust would arrive quickly. I would prepare myself for the back of my t-shirt to flicker in the wind and the cold chill to run down my neck. It was a similar feeling to when I capsized in the river where rolling up caused water to trickle down my neck making my spine tingle. The feelings made me want to close my eyes, shake and moan. I knew that would not help my situation: whenever I closed my eyes my shoulders would raise up tensioning my whole back. Controlling this natural reaction was hard, my brain was tired and slow but I had to remember I had damaged my neck in some way. My native instinct of protection and survival meant I did my best not to shake and tried to not tense up but it was inevitable.

The wind also heightened other noises which I had been blissfully unaware of. So far in the night, I had not really paid attention to the sounds. They had not seemed that important, the only sounds I had focused on were my own breaths and my heart beat. Now these new noises were scary and they were intensified by the early morning darkness and shadows. I was exhausted and my mind had been consumed by so many fears, I had not considered the wildlife around me. What animals could be out there? Would they eat me? Was that to be my fate, be eaten slowly alive by some native mammal to this area? I wish I had paid more attention to Sam and asked what animals were out here. I had to steady myself before I let myself get carried away. Fortunately, I am not a person scared of spiders, mice or small rodents. However, in the dark of the night a concealed rustling noise behind you became eerie. My immobility left me feeling vulnerable and images from the films 'Predator' and 'Alien' rushed through my mind. I began talking to myself: "Come on Gilly, get a grip."

My world of steam train rhythm shaking, along with the rain and the heavier gusts of wind were more than my mind could cope with. The thought of animals and being eaten flew out with the same speed it had come in with. All I could do to calm myself was, take myself back to the basics. So I spoke to myself inside my head and counted aloud; "Breathe in for one", I sucked in the cold air through my mouth. "Then breathe out for two. One. Two. Breathe in for one. Then breathe out for two. One. Two." This continued and after a little while became automatic once more.

Light shaded the valley and slowly the silhouettes I'd been surrounded by gathered details. The morning before the mountain had been an amazing place. The new colours, the smells, even the way the soil felt between my toes had been a source of excitement. Now it was all too much. I couldn't raise any interest in it. I wanted nothing more than to be away from it. My eyes scanned around me at the revealed ridges, crags and trees and I wished myself home. The only useful thing I could make of it was that the trees, at the top of the ridge in front of me, would sway with the gusts. The rain began to chill me again. Now that I had successfully turned myself back onto my side I curled back into the foetal position and the world went silent once more for me.

After what seemed to be another age the silence gave way to a whirling sound. It got steadily closer and louder, penetrating my pain and misery. I couldn't work out what it was. I knew it wasn't the wind. It wasn't an animal either. I felt a deep lethargy. The pain and I were now used to each other, it was just something that was a constant. There was a slight increase in temperature but nothing to raise my spirits. I wanted to sleep and was drifting in and out of it. The whirling noise became more insistent and I looked up to see a helicopter passing a ridge in the distance. I had become detached from reality. I thought about how nice it would be to take a helicopter ride and see the sunrise over the mountain from the air. It took me back to a dream I had had of taking a helicopter ride over and then into the Grand Canyon, and how amazing it would be to see such an awe inspiring natural wonder of the world. This dream was only a few days ago. I continued to watch the helicopter with interest; it was the first thing to take my attention in many hours. It hovered over the top of the mountain for a while and then began sweeping the side of it. I was confused; I questioned why someone would want to take a ride and do that, I couldn't see the point in it. I certainly wouldn't pay for that type of ride. Then it dawned on me, it could be looking for someone. Perhaps it was me. There was a small gleam of hope that lit up in me, but I didn't let it grow very brightly. I resigned myself to thinking it would be nice if it was, but I wasn't going to lay any bet on it.

I drifted away again. This sleep was different from the lighter sleeps I had taken in the night. I had fought against those sleeps. They were dangerous; they challenged my will to live and threatened my future. This one drew me in. It offered me peace. I wanted it to wrap me up; to take away the pain from my bones, sooth my tired eyes. I had been completely alone for hours. I had worked hard to control my panic, my thoughts, the pain that was racking my body and the cold. I was ready to relinquish control and that was incomprehensible; it has always been a measure of weakness to me. I didn't know how to move on from this moment. There seemed to be nothing to do so I chose to do nothing.

The sleep was deep and comforting. I drifted in and reluctantly out of it. My pain was easing and my eyes refused to open. Every so often I could hear the buzz of the rotors as the helicopter passed nearby, perhaps looking in neighbouring gullies, never near enough to find me. Why would they? They had been looking for so long and hadn't found me. Why would they succeed this time? My past experiences of help had left a bad taste in my mouth and the negative was all that I could feel. I dearly wanted someone to wrap me up in their arms and comfort me. I knew that wouldn't work, the pain had affected my soul and any safe place I once had, had long gone. I was angry inside; angry that I had nothing left to give or hope for. All I knew was that the only person I could rely upon was me and right now there wasn't much of me to do that either. All that was left was sleep and nothing else to do, so I gave myself over to it. I felt my body slip away, the pain was going and I could hear voices comforting me.

I don't know what woke me up. Perhaps it was the t-shirt wrapped around my head slipping off, but suddenly I was back in the world and I could see the helicopter. It was in the gully next to me. I had unconsciously been taking note which gullies it had been in and knew it must be due to check mine at some point soon. I didn't want to get my hopes up but some form of statistics had to come into my favour at some point, didn't they? It was too far away and I knew that if it began to survey the area that I was in, I needed to get its attention. I watched the light it was using to scan and how it seemed to pan each little nook and cranny for ages. My mind shifted from its negative state almost instantaneously to one which had hope. There was hope in there, I was not dead yet and I certainly intended to die trying to be seen. The helicopter came slowly towards me. I couldn't believe my eyes. What felt like hours had passed since my first glimpse of it. Time began to accelerate back towards its normal pace.

My bloodstained white tank top was beside me and my body seemed to fill with energy. My mind had drawn strength from some unknown place. I picked the top up with an ease of movement I hadn't felt at any time that night and began waving it above my head with my right hand. For a moment the movement was hard, but then the helicopter moved a little in my direction and I felt a tremendous surge of strength. I waved and waved my t-shirt and at the same time began saying in my head "Help, I'm here. Before I knew it I was saying it out loud. Each time I said it, made me believe this was reality and it was actually happening. The helicopter came closer, its pilots focussed on a circle of light below it. I could see the pilots. The first people I had seen since Mike had left. I almost wanted to pinch myself to confirm what was happening, but there was no time to waste.

The downdraft of the helicopter increased as it came closer to where I was located. I knew I would only have one chance and I racked my brains to find a way to make my small body more visible when it came over me. I was sure that I would just have the one chance. I had to get myself from lying on my side to at least sitting, that way I could potentially use two hands to wave. I thought to myself, could I manage to stand? I would be able to make myself much much bigger that way. I began my manoeuvre; I knew I had little time to do it. As the helicopter swivelled its search light towards me, I was almost onto my feet. The blood stained tank top in my right hand waving frantically, my left arm waving up and down.

The helicopter was now right in front of me. Everything around me was starkly lit by its searchlight and I could see the pilots clearly and the orange lights reflecting off things in their cockpit. They felt close enough to touch but yet still just out of reach. The down draft beat my clothing and time stood still. I was screaming "Help" at the pilots. I was screaming for my life, with every emotion I could muster to make myself as loud as possible. There is a certain desperation you can hear when someone scream s for help and really means it; I meant it with all my heart and soul. I could see their eyes but I knew that they couldn't see mine. Gradually the helicopter moved on.

My one chance had gone. To have them come that close and then to go away and leave me was too much to bear. I lost control of my emotions. I could no longer bear the thought of being stuck in this place. I screamed my impotent rage at the sky. Why hadn't they seen me?

I collapsed from my almost upright position, the exertion had taken its toll on my weak body but more so on my mind. I gazed at my feet and saw the backpack that Mike had left beside me. Inside it was a packet of crisps. It had a foil lining that would reflect light better than the blood stained top, why hadn't I gone for that? There was also my camera, why hadn't I got that out. I shouted at myself, "stupid, stupid girl!" I was swallowed up in my own depression, unable to look away from my feet. Tears swamped my eyes and made my feet look blurry. I was in my own bubble, but the bubble no longer had any protection. It was just me exposed on the mountain and I could no longer take it. I begged and shouted out to be swallowed up into a big hole.

The helicopter flew away from me.

I was devastated. Negativity engrossed me. I saw the helicopter as my last resort in being rescued. Through my blurred vision from the tears, I glanced at the ground below me. The only way for me to survive is if I do it myself. I had to get myself down to the bottom, down to civilisation. From childhood, I had learnt to rely upon myself, I was fiercely independent. I was angry, cross and was in a rage. I rarely ever asked for help, so why when I screamed for it, had it gone. The rage drove me to try to get to my feet once more, tears running down my face, my hands clenched with the pain. I couldn't get up, but I would make it down off this mountain and live. I began to shuffle forwards on my bottom. I was rewarded with massive shooting pains in my pelvis. I nearly collapsed in agony. I put my hands over my face and willed myself to control the pain. There was so much I wanted to do with my life. I wanted a second chance with my family. I wanted to make a better job of communicating with them, to put things right. I had so much to do, there had to be a better purpose for my life than a one day headline for the news services in New Mexico. I was desperate to stay alive.

At that moment the helicopter came back into sight, a man already swinging down on the winch wire, coming towards me. I could barely believe what was happening. Was I actually about to be rescued? I half fell back on to the ground. For a brief moment I was alone again, shivering in the enormous downdraft of the helicopter blades. I thought the sheer power of it would break my teeth, and then the winch man was scrambling up towards me. I wiped my tears from my eyes with my grubby hands in readiness to greet this person. He was a dark silhouette moving towards me and as he got closer I could make out a face. When he was about two metres away I could see him taking in deep breaths, I couldn't hear anything under the drone of the helicopter. At that moment, I did not care about that.

A metre away from me, I could make out his features of his face. His mouth opened, "I bet you're glad to see me," were his first words. I could have kissed him, but I just smiled.

"Yeah, it gives me someone else to talk to." He smiled back at me and got out his radio. It was such a relief to actually speak to someone. He started scanning me up and down and I watched with intrigue whilst trying to control the shaking. The helicopter was still whirling above us making the cool air even colder.

"She's alive and in good spirits" he reported into his radio. He began checking my obvious damage and asked where else it hurt.

"My neck and my leg," I replied, but I'm not sure whether he heard me. The helicopter was very noisy. It was hard for me to hear him and I know I wasn't very loud. My inner desire to make myself believe this wasn't as serious a situation and I was not as hurt as I knew I was came across once more.

"Let's patch you up a bit," he said, before turning away. "I've just got to go and get something."

"You can't leave me." I was afraid that if I let him out of my sight the whole wait would start again.

"I'm not leaving you," he promised and came back immediately with a first aid pack and began to apply dressings to my head and leg. Time seemed to be flying past: before I knew it the dressing was on my leg. It felt quite loose, I tried to adjust it with my fingers but they were cold and were pretty useless. My hands felt more like claws. My rescuer was too busy with trying to put a dressing on my head to care that the one on my leg was loose. He seemed in a rush to get them on and I felt rushed as well. I was embarrassed by my inability to move my body quickly and wanted to show my rescuer my willingness to get off the mountain quickly, but mind and body were not working together which just added to my frustration. I didn't have a chance to dwell on it for long.

"Can you walk?" he asked.

"No." I didn't have any doubts about that.

"OK. We can get a stretcher down or you can go up on a pod."

"Whichever is quickest," I shouted, fighting to be heard above the drone of the helicopter blades. My mind was still running at a hundred miles an hour, even if my body wasn't. It was protecting me, as even though I was trying not to show it to my rescuer, I knew deep down I could not keep going for much longer. The longer I tried to hold this front, that all was fine, the more precious energy I was using. He spoke into his radio again and a large three legged pod came down from the helicopter. I initially attempted to ease myself onto the pod, but I just could not move myself. I gazed into my new friend and he seemed to look straight through me. Before I could even yelp with pain, he had lifted and straightened out my right leg, so it went over one of the legs and did the same with my left. My bottom was now perched on the third prong. He wrapped a strop around me and, attached the bag to the other side. Within a few moments the wire went tight and my legs began to dangle below me. As I left the mountain, I looked down at my rescuer as I spun around a little. I didn't dare look out in front of me. I was too scared and worried about the consequences of falling again. I had to think positively and leave my anxiety on the ground. I was in the air moving swiftly towards the helicopters rails, I was on my way back to life.

# 5 BACK FROM THE DEAD

"I've never been in a helicopter before. This is quite exciting.

"If we had a bit more time we'd give you a bit of a tour." With that my saviour clamped a set of ear defenders on my head.

It's a bizarre conversation to be having with your rescuers but, as ever, I was putting a brave face on it. I was scrunched over into a corner of the helicopter fuselage with my legs straight out in front of me and webbing on the walls supporting my back. I was pushing myself up with my hands because putting weight on my bottom was painful. I knew something was broken but I didn't know what. As the winchman closed the door the helicopter tilted, showing me the mountainside below. I felt my stomach swoop and tried to push myself further back, away from the risk of falling back out.

The flight was very short. The inside of the helicopter was dark and I began to drift into a dream world. We only seemed to be in the air for seconds. I was still controlling the shivers with my breathing. The inside of the helicopter felt far warmer which started to warm me up. We landed on a long strip of tarmac that I thought was a runway, but which turned out to be a closed highway. The rotors clattered to a stop and the winchman climbed out. Able to hear again, one of the pilots turned around and offered me a drink of water. He was good looking, with well defined cheekbones. I remember thinking that he must be muscular.

"I'd love some. I must look a mess" He loosened the lid and handed me a bottle.

"I've seen better," he said, as I took the water. The inside of the helicopter was dark and the doorway created a magnificent window showcasing the outside world. The world I had been doing everything in my power to be a part of, but rather than feeling a part of it, I just felt like I was looking at it from afar. Part of me was in it, but a big proportion of me was merely looking at it as if it was a picture and I was holding its frame. The mountain I had been on and thought I would never come off, filled the skyline of the picture. The sun had not fully risen in the sky and there were still dark shadows filling the bottom of the picture.

I shuffled myself towards the doorway. The world outside was bright and hurt my eyes. It was liberating and I felt free, as I was now sitting on the edge of the helicopter with my legs hanging over the edge. I could feel them swing a little below me. "I bet you're glad to be down."

"Oh, massively; that was one long, long night."

I was in a surreal place, flirting with the pilot, sitting on the edge of a picture frame world and watching as an ambulance raced up to us. A paramedic came over and began checking my dressings. The one on my leg felt like it was now around my ankle rather than on my shin. Whether it was or not, I have no idea as all I could see was the world ahead of me. A stretcher was produced from the ambulance and brought close, but not up to the helicopter.

"Can you walk?" It was the second time I had been

asked this question and my compulsion to pretend everything was fine was still strong. The fact I knew something was wrong with my neck was put aside once more, along with the pain I was in. I felt as if I should at least try to attempt to walk because I didn't want to be a bother and make a fuss. To show I needed help was not something I was used to doing and strong Gilly was out and showing her stubbornness.

"I don't know; I can try." The medic and pilot took hold of my arms and we tried walking. I don't remember putting many steps in before they hoisted me up and shuffled me over to the stretcher. They dropped the bed and I was spun around, so I could sit on it. I turned on my left leg while my right leg dragged along the floor and did not do what I expected it to do. My body felt rigid and to be able to bend it in half and sit felt completely unnatural. The relief of being rescued and the adrenaline were wearing off. Even that small effort, from the helicopter to the stretcher, was a major undertaking and my whole body ached and felt really heavy. They asked me to lie down but I couldn't. The rugby ball lump I had forgotten about was now making itself felt again. I was shouting with the pain as they swung my legs up. Once there, the lump felt as if it was deflating, like a balloon and it hurt less, but lying flat was unbearably uncomfortable. The slightest movement sent pain up my body and down my legs in lightning bolts. The screams of pain I was letting out did not deter the paramedic and I felt like a small child who was crying over a small insignificant graze. The next thing I knew we were in the ambulance and moving. The dream world went away and everything accelerated. They asked my name and began to explore where I was hurting. I don't remember being able to give them my name. Everything was happening so quickly; my brain and mouth were not working in harmony. I was so cold, my teeth were chattering so badly that getting out words was very difficult. They covered me in blankets that felt as if they had been in an oven. I tried to compose myself and in between the groans of pain, I yelled "The blankets are burning me!"

"No they aren't." There was a rushed feeling in the air once again. .It felt as if things needed to be done quickly, but there were barriers in the way. I am good at reviewing options and making rapid decisions. I hate the feeling that I'm not contributing, but this time, unlike when I was on the mountain with my rescuer, all I could do was lie there, helpless. A medic tried to put a cannula into my hand and I heard him call through to the cab for advice.

"I can't get a line in." He turned his attention back to me. "Where are you hurting?"

It sounded in my head as if I was whispering as I didn't want to really admit to it. I told him I had pain in my hips, my back and then I mentioned my neck.

Everything suddenly became a lot more serious. His hands went straight to my neck, immobilising my head as he called another medic through from the front, urgently. They stopped the ambulance and cut my clothes away to put me into a neck brace. I think I blacked out then. The next thing I remember there was a bang as the stretcher went through a set of double doors. There were lots of people around me. It was like an episode of a medical drama. I don't remember their faces. I only have flashes of memory from my day in the Emergency Room. I owe my life to so many people who flit through my consciousness like shadows. Between the drugs and the exhaustion I cling to the knowledge that they are the reason I am alive and can walk today. They gave me my second chance at life, although it took me a little time to realise it.

"We have a white female, twenty years old, she's hypothermic and we can't get any lines in. We've tried..."

It was almost as if I wasn't there, but watching myself on the television. There were all kinds of unexplained noises and lots of people wanted my attention. Although I was there and it was me they were talking about, my mind and body were still somewhat disconnected. All I really wanted to do was sleep. After a while a medic seemed to have been assigned to look after me. He was very patient and questioned me gently. He asked what the day was. Such a simple question yet I couldn't quite place it. My mind was working very slowly. I knew that I should know but I needed time to work it out. I explained that because I didn't have a watch I shouldn't be expected to come with the answer straight away. I went through an elongated tale of my visit to the Grand Canyon and our walks before I eventually arrived at Thursday. It made the medic laugh and we shared a moment of triumph. It didn't help that I couldn't move my hands. He stayed with me for a while. He was very calm and he seemed to be trying to connect with me so that I would trust him. It made the situation less scary. He quickly read that I needed simple explanations and gave me them.

They moved and manipulated me. A sudden flash made me jump which they told me was an x-ray. I could hear them discussing my injuries.

"There's a break here, and a clear fracture there." I heard them mention the Sacro-Iliac joint.

My need to still make it known I was here and alive, compelled me to join in the conversation.

"Ooh," I said, "I know what that joint is."

"Really?" My new friend asked.

"Oh yes," I replied, "I'm studying Sports Science." They were trying to keep me talking and conscious but we began a conversation on sports. My jovial side came out. In the night I had suffered from weakness and the erosion of hope. That despair had been replaced by a desperate desire to be out of the Hospital. I had to be strong. If I could be strong and convince them that there was nothing seriously wrong with me I could get out and get back to my life. It was time for my tougher persona, Strong Gilly, to make a reappearance. I was still cold but I wasn't hurting anymore, so my brain told me that obviously I was not that seriously hurt and I could go home fairly soon. The more realistic reason was that they must have managed to give me some kind of pain relief. They wanted to put a catheter in and explained that they wanted to give my body the minimum possible to think about. At the time I had no comprehension as to what a catheter was or meant. So I asked if I could sleep and was told no. My cheeks dropped a little with the answer, so I did my best to stay awake and I listened in as much as possible to what was being said around me. Apparently my stats were low and my heart rate was high.

"Did you say my heart rate was high?" I was concerned. "I know what my resting rate is."

"Do you. What's that?"

"It's normally about forty"

"It's a hundred and forty at the moment." It was a reminder of just how serious my situation was. I was beginning to panic a bit. The seriousness of the situation was becoming more apparent. You could tell the medics were taking it seriously as there were a lot of voices all around me working on different bits of me. I had to accept that I knew my body was a bit of a mess. I wasn't allowed to move or do anything. They gave me morphine for the pain and after that I don't remember much. Time began to move in and out of focus. I asked to see the x-ray of my pelvis and my friend showed me it. He pointed out the four separate fractures and how they might impact on me.

"That makes sense," I said, "that's why it hurts. But there are no bones sticking out, are there?"

"No, no, we can't see any bones." My question seemed to amuse him.

"Are you sure, because that's what it feels like."

"No, we'll give you more pain relief."

During another more lucid moment I heard a very jolly person come in.

"Did you hear about the walker who fell on the Sandia Mountain last night? I think we might see her at some point. The radio said she'd been rescued."

I paused as I took this information in. It hadn't occurred to me that my predicament would have reached the attention of the media. Little did I realise the extent to which it had.

"I guess that's me, then." The room went a little quiet. Someone else came in and told them that my friends were here and wanted to see me.

"We can't allow that. We have to get her stable first."

"What's stable?" I don't remember getting an answer. I was moved several times, but eventually I came to rest in a room of my own.

Mike was the first one allowed in to see me. I don't remember much about it, just the touch of his hand on mine and then he seemed to go again. A nurse wheeled me off in my bed for more scans. I was struggling with the pain again. It was unbearable as they moved me from the bed onto a solid scanner board. I was begging for padding. In one scanner they were delighted and surprised to find that I hadn't broken either leg.

"At least I did one thing right!" The moments of humour were essential. The more scans and x-rays they sent me for, the more I was frightened. Eventually I seemed to be back in my room. Sam was allowed in and it was as if she could see right through me. I tried to be brave but she could see how scared I was. She knew she couldn't say anything to me that would help, so she went to work on the staff. I had had enough of being prodded and all I wanted was for the pain to go. Sam pleaded on my behalf to take me off the spinal board but they weren't having any of it. All I wished for was more padding to provide some comfort. Mike joined us and asked for my Mum's phone number and he had the unenviable task of calling her.

A short while later a nurse came in and told me that

Mum was on the phone. They put the phone to my ear.

"Hello. I hear you've had a bit of an accident."

"Yes. I'm sorry."

As I heard my Mums voice for the first time, it released something in me; I began to cry. I hadn't thought about my Mum since moving myself into my foetal position on the mountain. I wanted that hug more than anything now; I needed to rekindle positive memories that had been destroyed. It brought home to me how much of a mess I was in and just how far from home. Strong Gilly, however, was never far from control and she wanted to put a brave face on it and didn't want to worry her.

"Don't apologise, these things happen. I thought I'd better find out how you are. Mike told me, but I thought I'd better get it from you. If you wanted me to come to New Mexico, you only had to ask!" Because she was talking to me normally it helped. She went on tell me how she had been icing a cake. I didn't really know how much was wrong with me then, so we played it down. I told her not to come over. When she put the phone down I cried again. Seeing how upset I was the nurse sat with me and held my hand for a while. Afterwards she worked in the background, always letting me know that she was there and would give me time whenever I needed it.

A lovely young man came in to take me down for an MRI Scan. It seemed to be a very long ride along deserted corridors. We began to talk: he was a medical student working as a porter to help pay his way through college. He was also a sports fanatic and played soccer for the University. Because I'd played a lot at school we had plenty to talk about. When we finally arrived I was reluctant to let him leave me and he promised that he would wait and take me back. I was very tired; they told me I could sleep as I went through the machine, although it might be hard with the noises it was going to make. I didn't have any trouble and dozed off quite quickly. Eventually they finished scanning and photographing me.

My chauffeur loaded me back onto my mobile bed and prepared to take me away.

"Can I go back to sleep?" I asked.

"I was hoping we could talk more about soccer." Without realising it, he had hooked me back into a conversation that I loved to have with Americans. I'd had many similar discussions at summer camp.

"It's called football. You have a ball that you hit with your foot. What else could it be called?" It made him laugh but the argument didn't last long as I drifted back into sleep.

I don't really remember them giving me the results. It wasn't good, though. I had fractured my pelvis in four places. It was difficult but not impossible to deal with. There was some discussion that it may need fixing but at that point, I didn't know what fixing meant and apparently it was not the priority. More seriously I had fractured my C4 vertebra and dislocated C5 and C6. This was frightening territory. Any damage to the spinal column in the high cervical nerve area (C1-4) can lead to tetraplegia, almost complete paralysis. It usually means breathing difficulties, 24 hour a day care and can even takeaway your ability to speak. It was a miracle I hadn't done more damage to my spinal column with all my bouncing and efforts to climb in and out of helicopters. In order to realign my vertebrae and prevent further damage they told me that I would need an operation. I really didn't want that. I was strong Gilly, I could heal myself. I was an athlete with my first International Competition to get to. I refused it.

I was told that there were no other options; that I really needed the operation if I was to walk again, let alone compete but I was adamant. I may even have been a little paranoid. If I had an operation I would need recuperation time. They would cut me open and might put artificial parts inside me. Mum had had a number of operations and it seemed her body had suffered from being opened up lots of times. Her joints had less movement, which would mean I couldn't do all the things I loved. It would stop me from being so active. I absolutely hated the idea. During the debate a nurse brought me the news that Mum was on the phone again. Would I like to tell her the news about my neck?

All I really wanted was a hug, but Mum was thousands of miles away in England. Even if she had been with me the combination of neck brace, the spinal board and strapping down would have made it impossible. I settled for hearing her voice. This time her voice had a bit more of a worried tone in it, compared with the jovial first conversation. She could hear in my voice that I was scared and felt alone. We discussed my options and she helped me to accept that there were no options. I would have the operation. For the medics this decision must have signalled a frantic round of preparations. For me it meant another hiatus.

I was visited by another friend from camp, Anna-Marie, who distracted me with a View-Master picture show that didn't require me to move. It made me chuckle as it had pictures of Minnie and Mickey Mouse on. It was a good distraction. She was studying at the medical school and not only reassured me but was able to help me communicate with the medics. Mum called for a third time. By this stage, unbeknown to me, she had been plotting. She had spoken to my Dad and they were making arrangements to fly out to be with me. I didn't want to put anyone out. I had been silly and had a fall, but surely it didn't mean they had to put their lives on hold. Mum changed tack and told me that she had never been to America before. I began to enthuse about how much she would like it, how much she would enjoy the heat and the sunshine, the good the dryness would do for her health. I became obsessed with the need for her to use sun cream. It was enough. By the end of the phone call I had given them permission to come out. Not that I actually did have a choice on the matter, they were coming whatever. They were on the next available flight.

The Hospital swung back into action, I was becoming more stable and my body was slowly warming up. Now that they knew what was wrong they could start to fix the small stuff while they waited for a theatre for my spinal surgery. A very nice young man came and looked at my head wound. He told me that I had severed a nerve in my forehead and they would bring in a plastic surgeon to try to repair it. There was no guarantee it would be successful. If unsuccessful, it would mean that I would only be able to raise one eyebrow. He told me it could be quite cool. Lots of people work very hard to master the skill of lifting one eyebrow but I would be able to do it automatically. I don't know whether it was the relief of having made a decision, or whether the pain killers were making me high but this was the funniest thing I had heard for ages. He was about to make things worse.

"I have to put this green paper over your head and I think you're going to giggle." He read me correctly. I found it hysterical. I just couldn't stop laughing. After a short while he lifted it up again.

"Have you stopped yet?" There were tears of laughter rolling down my face. Whether it was the relief that this was the start of me being fixed or that I had gone through all other emotions. I am not sure, perhaps it was a bit of both but the laughter in itself was healing. As I laughed I could hear other people in the room laugh and that made the whole situation much easier to deal with. "OK, I'll just wait a few minutes while you get over it." I felt as if I was five years old and playing peek-a-boo. One of the girls was with me at the time and asking the important questions for me. It left me able to enjoy the experience. They cleaned me up and cut away some of my hair to make it easy to access the wound. As he was washing it I could feel the water washing across my skull and dribbling off my face. It set me off again.

Eventually they were all done and I was wheeled back to my room in the intensive care ward. Apparently I needed to be more stable before they would operate on my neck and they were going to wait until the next day. I was left alone with the girls and Mike. A little knowledge isn't always a good thing. I began to worry about what the next day would bring. At that moment I couldn't walk, I couldn't move any of my body. If the operation went wrong this could be my future. I had no energy and everything was being done for me. It was a horrible feeling. The girls did their best to keep my spirits up. A number of doctors came in to examine me and talk about the pending operation. They looked at my matted hair and I heard one of them say, they would need to shave it off. My hair was an important part of my identity. The girls saw the fear in my eyes so they captured a junior doctor and pleaded with him to lift my hair out from underneath my collar. Having just lost some to my scalp wound operation, I was paranoid about losing it all the next day. I was afraid that if I lost all my hair people wouldn't recognise me. I'm not much of a girly girl, my long hair is usually scraped back into a pony tail to keep it out of the way, but it mattered. The girls went to work on it for me, pulling out twigs and gently combing out the tangles. In reality they didn't achieve much but my mental state was lifted as I felt something positive was being done about keeping my identity.

Up until this summer I had spent a lot of my life hiding myself in identities that I hoped would fit in. I was strong Gilly for my family, helpful or academic Gilly at University and shy Gilly in social occasions. Somewhere in that past year, through working hard, competing at my paddling, from becoming a strong member of the team on the waterfront at camp and from creating instant and wonderful friendships in America I had become confident. I was the person I had always known I should be. I was just Gilly. In a few seconds of ricocheting down a mountainside I had lost all that. I couldn't move, let alone run or paddle; I had no energy even to speak. My bouncy pony tail seemed to be the only thing left of my happy confident personality and I was desperate not to lose it.

Sam, Kim and Jen worked hard and patiently on it for me, all the time talking to distract me, telling me the story of their long hard night waiting for news on the mountain, of the coverage I had received in the media (anonymous, because I had refused permission for the Hospital to release my name) and their joy at hearing the radio reports of my rescue. It was comforting, but I was only taking in snippets of the information in and I am sure they repeated themselves more than once. I was fading in and out of sleep.

When I woke it was silent and mostly dark in the room. I still couldn't move. It took a little while for me to place where I was, to realise that I wasn't back on the mountain. All I could see was the white of the ceiling and all I could hear was the bloop, bloop, bloop of the heart rate monitor; I couldn't work out what they were. I was devastated. I was no better off than I had been before. I had been alone on the mountain and now I was alone here. I began to repeat it, aloud. "I'm on my own. I can't be on my own. I can't move." I was hoping someone would respond. I just wanted to know that there was someone with me. I could move my hand a few centimetres but couldn't feel anything. I'd never been afraid of the dark before but now I couldn't bear it. I was getting into a real panic. The pain came back. It was getting worse by the second. Before long it was unbearable and this time I knew I wouldn't be able to stand it.

The destruction to my inner soul from being alone all night on the mountain had left me raw. All my defences had been pulled and torn down, then thrown up into the air. I had no more ways to deal with the pain. I no longer had happy or safe places to settle myself with. My world was now a very different place and all that was left was fear

47

and panic. Any sense of security I once had was left on the mountain.

Magically Sam appeared beside me. She had been asleep by my bed. It took her a long time to get through my fear, to begin to calm me down and to understand what was wrong. Just as she was making progress she announced that she would go for help. I couldn't bear the idea that she would leave me alone again. The last person to do that had been Mike and he hadn't come back. I clung on to her hand, but eventually she disentangled herself and left to get help. In a very short time the lights came on and the nurses arrived. They did observations but had nothing to offer in the way of pain relief. Sam went into overdrive and hounded the medical staff until a doctor was found who could take the pain away.

Sam became my guardian angel. I woke up several times that night. Every time I felt the same panic, began the same desperate search for contact and every time her hand immediately found mine, bringing me the comfort of knowing that I wasn't alone. That was when I realised that I could trust her. She wasn't going to go anywhere. The bond that had begun to develop in a cabin in Pennsylvania had become something much stronger here in New Mexico. We hadn't really known each other very well, but here I was at the lowest point in my life and she was always beside me. I was someone who kept their pain in, away from the eyes of the world and now I opened myself up to this girl who was my only lifeline. Mike was nowhere to be seen. I felt massively let down by him. But Sam was here and holding my hand when I needed it. It was a turning point. From the next morning I began pushing him away and brought the girls closer.

# 6 WITH A LITTLE HELP

The support of Sam, Kim and Jen both on the mountainside and in the Hospital was incredibly important to my survival. They put in more time and care than I could possibly have asked them for. They helped start rebuilding my life and during those first few days, created a safe place. They gave me light in a very dark tunnel throughout my early recovery. As a result we have become very close friends, despite living so far apart. I asked them for their memories of my time in Hospital.

SAM:

As soon as we knew that Gilly was safely on her way to Hospital we followed. They took her to the University Hospital. That was good for two reasons: firstly the doctors there are the very best in our town, and we knew she would have the best possible care; secondly my friends and I were students there at the time. We were going to be able to visit her easily.

When we arrived she was still in for her initial treatment and diagnoses. Mike was with her but no one else was allowed in. I was very worried for her. I was sure she would have hypothermia and shock but I had no idea what other injuries she might have from such a long fall.

We had to wait for about an hour but it seemed like forever.

When we were finally allowed to see her she looked awful. She was covered in dirt and blood and her hair was matted with twigs. She looked like a homeless woman who hadn't seen a bath for a week. To make things worse they had treated some of her obvious injuries and put her in a neck brace but the wound in her leg was so deep and had been open so long that they had delayed covering it until they could treat it properly. They had put her through all the scanners but at that time we were still waiting to know exactly what was wrong with her.

She was very shaken and stirred, but clearly relieved to be down from the mountain and in treatment. If anything she seemed a bit embarrassed about the trouble she had caused. Although she was worried about how badly she might be hurt, she clearly didn't think she merited all this fuss. It might have been the pain medication at work. I think I was in a worse state. I was sick to my stomach with an awful guilt. This had happened to her while she was staying with me and that made me feel responsible for it all.

Just after lunchtime they moved her out of ER and into a ward. By then they all knew that her neck was badly damaged and her pelvis was broken. She was pretty scared, but right from the start all she wanted was to get out and back to her life. I don't think I've ever seen such determination.

For the next few weeks life settled into a very crowded routine for Jen, Kim and I. We were all students at the University and the Hospital is on campus so we were able to visit easily, sometimes between lectures and tutorials. She was always impatient but, laying there immobilised, she went through all the stages of grief. We would talk through the options she had and she was very focussed – only a return to the life she had before the accident would do.

She was very afraid of being left alone. In her neck brace she couldn't turn her head and had nothing to occupy her. We would sit and hold her hand, reading to her. One day when she was very low we went to a party store and decorated her ceiling with a Hawaiian luau theme. When she was afraid it was very hard for me to be strong for her. A few years before this my mother had a stroke and in the process injured her neck. It has left her partially disabled and unable to do many things she previously took for granted. I worried constantly about how Gilly would manage if she was told she couldn't do the things she constantly talked about. I tried to distract her with talk of other options – things she might be able to do. I was worried that she wouldn't settle if she couldn't get back into boats and rivers. To their credit they never told her that she wouldn't.

When the doctors wanted Gilly to go to a rehab centre and she was determined to go straight home I was even more concerned. It was several weeks of therapy but I was sure it would make her stronger and increase her chances of getting her life back. A professional centre with physiotherapists would be certain to be more support than she could access at her parents' home. Typically determined and focussed Gilly would have none of it. She wanted t get back to her life and nothing would stop her.

She stayed for three nights at our friend Anna-Maria's home, where her parents had been staying while she organised her flight. This wasn't easy because of her medical requirements and needing enough room to lay down and Albuquerque only has a small airport. As soon as she came out and started working on this problem her spirits improved.

JEN:

Somehow you never expect to be sitting halfway up a mountain, waiting for news of a friend. I hadn't known Gilly long and didn't know her well but I took to her straight away. It was impossible not to like her. My sister and I had only just moved into a new apartment with Sam when she announced that her new friend Gilly would be arriving and staying with a friend for ten days. As we had no furniture at all I was a little worried but she loved camping with us in our empty rooms.

But then things went wrong. Living in Albuquerque you are already halfway up the mountain and whether you climb it or not you quickly learn about it. It can be an easy hike to the top when things go right, but weather conditions can easily make the desert trails hard to find and when that happens people regularly get into trouble. One of the State Policemen who stayed with us to coordinate the rescue was a nice young guy that I knew from a college class. We felt so helpless, waiting for news. There was trouble with helicopters and search areas because the lines from the Tram car crossed the search area. They wouldn't let Mike or any of us go back onto the mountain because of the darkness so all we could do was pester them for information. My State Policeman was very patient with us and knowing him really helped. He eventually helped us to get a National Guard helicopter with night imaging equipment assigned to the search.

Seeing Gilly in the Hospital wasn't as much of a shock for me as it was for Sam. Mike had already seen her before I was allowed in and he had warned me what to expect. She really did look as if she had tumbled down a mountain.

Although I didn't know Gilly very well to start with I happily took my turn looking after her in the Hospital. We were all at the University together and the campus was only a fifteen minute walk from our apartment. The Hospital was on campus so even though we all had heavy workloads from taking double classes we were able to spend a lot of time with her. We could dash from class to Hospital. We would sit with her and read from Harry Potter books. She really liked it. I would read to her until she fell asleep, then switch to the books I needed to study.

I had to keep reading them aloud because she would wake up if my voice stopped. She was terrified of being alone.

Things were clearly very difficult with Mike. He was still staying with us and spending as much time as he could in Hospital. He was really shaken up by the accident and wanted to help her but Gilly was pushing him away. It didn't help that they had talked before they went up the hill and he knew he wasn't going to be a part of her future. Then things got really stressful. I finished classes late one evening, somewhere around 9pm. I met Mike coming out. He told me that she had sent him away and that she didn't want anyone with her that night. I decided to go up anyway and, if asked, claim I hadn't seen him. She was very happy to see me and I spent the night there. She was clearly pushing him away. She had me change the passwords on her email account so that he couldn't help her with them. I sent an email for her to Paul, her paddling buddy, in which she played down her injuries. She tried very hard to present a strong front to the world.

She was always very determined to fix herself and get on with her life, but there were some very difficult nights where she worried about not walking again, let alone kayaking. We were the only ones who saw this. She wouldn't ever show her weakness to Mike.

Hanging out and talking really helped her. The more ridiculous and silly the conversation the better she seemed to do. It was clear that she didn't ever need to be alone. If there were rules about visiting the nurses were fabulous. They never ever kept us out and we were almost always able to have someone with her. She was never left alone, especially at night, we made sure one of us was with her, sometimes swapping in the early hours so that we would get some sleep. It was something we could do at nineteen. I'm not sure I could do it now.

There were some very bright young athletic doctors at the University Hospital. They encouraged her to get up and start moving again quickly. Here it's all about getting you up quickly to get on with your recovery.

The encouragement of the staff and support of my friends was very important to me in my recovery. As important was the fitness I had built up paddling kayaks and preparing to race. It gave me inner strength and passion for life without which I may never have been able to get myself to and out of Hospital in the manner I did.

# 7 FIRST STEPS

I took to canoeing from the first moment I sat in a boat. It was as if I had found my home. I was fourteen when Mum arranged my first canoe course as a reward for hauling tonnes of garden materials from the front to the back of the house. I was hooked from the very first day. I never seemed to have trouble understanding what to do. Unlike the sports we did at school where I really had to work hard to master the simplest skills, I was shown something once and seemed to just be able to do it. Any complex movement, like a javelin throw, meant that I had to think very hard to line up the movements in the right sequence and to remember which foot went where. Put a paddle in my hands, however, and I was off. It was very exciting. For the first time in my life I had found a place where I seemed to fit.

When I was quite young I was labelled as being very hyperactive. I had problems with almost any food affecting me. Some foods, like chicken gave me immense energy; others affected my joints and muscles badly. From being I was a toddler the whole family had to cope with my mood swings, sleeplessness, vomiting and screaming. Eventually a special diet with eight items on it made life easier for everyone. This made it difficult to eat away from home, but it didn't bother me. It just meant that I took my own food anywhere I went. In many ways I felt special.

My mother was married three times before I was twelve. These changes in father figure led me, unintentionally, to seek out people I could trust. Mum's second husband, to the best of my remembrance, was loving and patient. He was always there for me in my early years, and yet he left a massive scar on my childhood. He had mental health problems and became involved in some kind of fraud. He had not only used his own name, but the family name as well and left a lot of debt. Just after he left, we escaped for three very exciting months to New Zealand to visit my uncle, who had emigrated some years before. For several years we were rather short of money before Mum met husband number three. Initially things seemed better. He sold Superglue for a living and made Mum much happier. When Mum was happier we were all happier. I remember Mum, Claire and husband number three all managing to stick themselves together with Superglue and feeling jealous at being left out of the giggling.

School wasn't any easier for me. I had difficulty making friends with girls in my classes and struggled to keep up with the reputation that Claire had made for herself. She was very bright and most of the teachers knew her. I found the comparisons difficult and tried hard to compete with her. I looked up to her and admired her; I wished I could be more like her. I began to have difficulty communicating. I wanted to tell my Mum how lonely and different I found myself at school, but I just couldn't find the words. When my Mum asked me what was wrong everything I wanted to say turned into blankness. She would become angry at my silence and I would close up even more. I began to take refuge in my room, communicating by means of black looks and talking to the walls.

I became very angry and agitated.  I was being teased at school, either as a boffin for studying hard or for playing football with the boys.  I began to build walls in my head to protect myself.  I needed time with my Mum, but when I got it I couldn't communicate how I felt.  Husband number three tried to help but I couldn't bring myself to trust him.  I lived largely in my own little bubble, dreaming of sporting success or making and selling rhubarb ice-cream.  It got worse when husband number three's son came to live with us for a while.  It felt as if Claire and I became the outsiders in his neat little family.  His son had a lot of problems at school.  He was dyslexic, badly behaved and told lies.  One morning he was chased down the stairs by his father.  I didn't know what had caused it, but suddenly the two were kicking and punching each other in our living room.  He was stuck in a corner and appeared to be egging his Dad on.  I was terrified and hid behind the sofa, but Claire tried to separate them.  She was pushed to one side.  He left soon after that.  The situation left me feeling shocked and ashamed at myself for hiding.  I vowed to myself I would never do that again.  Since that day I have always stepped in to help where I can.  It has brought me many friends.

This disruption at home taught me to hide my feelings.  I didn't tell anyone my troubles and it came to a head one day when my whole class seemed to be laughing at me.  I walked out of class and had to be coaxed out of the toilets.  That afternoon I was called out of a lesson to the Assistant Head's office, where I found my Mum and husband number three and I was recommended to see a psychologist.  It didn't help much.  My conversations with her just seemed to go around in circles and I never could get close to the cause of my problems.  She suggested a family therapy session but it went badly from the start.  I felt flattened and closed down again.  We discontinued the sessions shortly afterwards.  It reinforced for me that I had to rely on myself to find solutions.

My brother, Josh, was born when I was thirteen. I loved him from the first time I saw him and Claire and I helped out as much as we could; often taking over completely when Mum's health was poor. I badly needed an outlet and then, at the age of fourteen, Mum sent me on a canoeing course as a reward for helping with a new patio. That's when things began to improve; I had found a small solution!

The course took place in the pool at our local sports centre. It had what I now know to be an unusual programme. We were taught safety first, capsizing and exiting the boat. Then they taught us to scull for support. This is a little used advanced skill that requires you to balance the boat on edge, at 90 degrees, and support it on a paddle blade sculling across the surface of the water. It's a bit like stroking the water with a knife as if to butter it. If you have it at the wrong angle you cut the bread; in a boat you loose stability and end up totally upside down. It isn't an easy skill to learn. Most people struggle with it because getting it wrong usually means that you capsize and, as a beginner, swim. I thought it was natural and I quickly mastered it.

When the course came to an end I used my own money to sign up immediately to do an advanced course the following week. My instructor wasn't impressed. She was sure that it would be too hard for me, but I was determined to prove her wrong. My stubbornness came through and I loved the second week too. It seemed that everything she told us to do I was able to do very quickly. People often have trouble picking up some of the elements of canoeing. There are a lot of factors that can impede learning – fear of falling in, difficulty controlling the direction of the boat – but it seemed to come naturally to me. Anything our coach asked us to do I just did.

I had a really enjoyable and exciting time but that might have been the end of it. Soon after we went back to school, however, a notice appeared offering a new after school canoe club. I jumped at the chance to go. John Scales was a new maths teacher who was only at the school for a year or so. He was a real enthusiast who really loved paddling. Once we got to know him he would spend any spare moment talking about paddling, even sitting with us at lunchtime. He was very encouraging but I do wonder whether I developed as a paddler faster than he could keep up with.

On the first session, he asked me what I had done and I had trouble explaining. I hadn't been given any names for the skills we had learned at the pool. The only way was to show him. He checked our ability to safely get out of the boat and then gave the group paddles. I was off. Towards the end of the session he said "Do you want to try a roll?"

"What's that?" I replied.

"Oh, one of these," he said, and demonstrated one. Then one of the sixth formers demonstrated to. By the end of the session I had rolled my boat. I didn't know it at the time, but most people don't learn to roll that quickly. At the end of my first term I could do a pawlata roll, using the end of the paddle to gain more leverage, a screw roll – the kind of roll that is really useful on a river and the beginnings of hand rolling. By the end of the third session I could roll consistently in the pool but it took a lot longer to be useful on a river.

After a couple of months Mr Scales asked if I would like to do more paddling and whether I would like to get out onto a real river. At that moment there was nothing I wanted more. For the first time it felt as if something was working for me. He gave me some contact details for the local canoe club and Mum gave them a ring. She organised for me to go down to a session on the River Chelmer.

At that time Chelmsford Canoe Club had a distinct focus on racing. When I turned up it seemed no one was really expecting me. After some delay Alex, one of the racing team, found a boat and popped me in it. It was a Wavehopper, a plastic racing boat which was all she knew how to use. It was nothing like the big pool boats I had been used to. It had a long, thin hull shape. I later learned that it was designed to be very fast through moving water. All I knew was that it was very unstable. I was quite scared of falling in but I knew that this was something I really wanted to do. I must have demonstrated my ability to her because after a while she transferred me into a more stable boat and I was allowed to join the advanced group.

All that winter I paddled with the club. Every Saturday morning we trained in racing boats. They tried to get me to participate in marathon canoe racing, but I had no interest whatsoever in it. I only got excited when the water was up and it had some flow in it. However, the training did provide me with an excellent skill base in forward paddling that was useful later. The trouble was that I wasn't really interested in going fast in a straight line. I wanted adventure and I was getting bored. Sometimes an instructor called Bill took us out and showed us some other skills (other than going in a straight line). I was in awe of the effortless way he manoeuvred his boat. It made me feel as if I was in a big bath tub. I knew that the club did trips to paddle white water but I always seemed to miss out on the limited number of places there were on the trips. Without progression I was beginning to lose interest. What I wanted was to paddle in plastic boats; surf on the weir, play and have fun. I didn't find just going up and down the river exciting.

One incident turned things around for me. In the summer Mr Scales took a sixth former and I out to assess us for the British Canoe Unions (BCU) Two Star Kayak skills test. This is a personal skills national award scheme where there are five levels, the difficulty of skills increases exponentially. I failed on only two skills, both of them as performed on the left side of the boat (my weaker side). I had no problem with the rest of the skills. I went back to the canoe club and asked for help. I approached Carl Foody, one of the club's white water coaches who ran a summer recreation session on Wednesday evenings. Of medium height and very athletic, Carl is a very chilled and relaxed character. He is also a massive optimist. I was used to people around me who always saw trouble coming and Carl was a complete change, he rarely sees the negative in a situation and he has a very calming presence. He's a very smooth paddler, his boat moves effortlessly. I couldn't see how he did it and wanted to be able to paddle the way he could.

He asked me to join him the next week so that he could take a look at me. I think that he had already picked me out as having potential from the trouble my restlessness was causing the racing coaches. Mr Scales came along too and they had me go through everything I knew. Carl showed me some new skills and I picked them up quite easily. This gave me more confidence in my ability and I was able to brace effectively on both sides. Then they asked me to demonstrate some more skills, that hadn't been in my first test. At the end of the session Carl handed me a pass slip and told me to send it off.

"Congratulations," he said, "you've passed your Three Star Kayak."

I was astonished. At that time the British Canoe Union described the Three Star Test as the definition of a paddler. Carl explained that I was way above the standards required for a Two Star and only a little weak on the new skills he had passed on to me that day. Mr Scales asked me not to talk about it at school, explaining that there were older pupils working towards Three Star who would be upset to find that I had got there first.

At the Canoe Club it made a big difference. With my Three Star I was deemed responsible. That summer I was permitted to take people out onto the water. I started right away and began to build a group of rebel recreational paddlers who, like me, didn't want to do flat water paddling, but wanted to play and learn what our boats could do on moving water. We had a wonderful time, even if we were frowned upon, a little, by the racing paddlers. I also began to paddle with Carl's group. His can-do attitude rubbed off on me and I improved quickly.

When I went back to school things were changing. Mr Scales had moved on to another school and left a coaching vacuum which meant the after school club stopped for a year. It didn't stop me progressing with my own paddling. I decided I wanted to become a coach. I made enquiries at Chelmsford Canoe Club and they were delighted. They helped me to find courses and, in quick succession, I did the Canoe Safety Test, a First Aid course and then a coaching course to become a Trainee Level Two Coach. Once I was qualified, I was asked to start the after school club as I was now in my final year of sixth form. I threw myself into the new challenge at school. I even took some of my teachers canoeing but I soon began to struggle. With my limited experience I couldn't control people in the pool at all. The games we played on the river were of no use in the pool and my lack of experience really showed. I didn't know anything about group control or linking together sessions. The school decided that I was unsafe and brought in another coach to mentor me.

This had a devastating effect on my self confidence that was already ebbing. To make things worse they brought in the coach from my first canoeing course to supervise me. She checked and approved my lesson plans. The whole experience left me feeling a failure and hating coaching. I knew that I was a better paddler than she was. Her paddling techniques and coaching methods were very out of date, but she could run a session much better than I could. I knew I had to prove myself and show that I could really coach.

Help turned up at Chelmsford Canoe Club. Paul Anderson, another of the club's coaches, took me under his wing. Paul's energy and enthusiasm make him appear like a huge puppy dog, but don't be fooled. He has a razor sharp intelligence and knows exactly what he wants. He can switch in an instant from jovial and fun to serious and in control and then back again when the need has passed. He was twenty seven when I was first introduced to him and he was one of the BCU's National Wild Water Racing coaches. He had had a distinguished paddling and racing career; he had paddled internationally in the canoe Marathon Team and Wild Water Team, and run some very challenging big water first descents in South America. As a coach he had already taken paddlers to World Championships.

He made a deal with me: he would teach me to become a coach if I would try Wild Water Racing. He put me back in my first nemesis boat; a Wavehopper. We went for a paddle and, as we came back to the bank, he told me to roll it.

"You what?" I said.

"Roll it!" He pushed my shoulder gently and the thin tippy boat went straight over. By now I was adept at it and rolled it straight back up.

"And again," he said.

"You what?" I barely got the words out before I was over again. He made me roll it three times before we got off the river. After that I was invited to join his paddling group. There were about seven of us paddling and training in Wild Water Racing boats every Tuesday. They were a lively bunch, full of banter which was new to me. It gave me a massive confidence boost. It wasn't quite enough.

In November Paul and Carl took me for my first white water weekend. Finally, at the age of seventeen, I would be able to go on something I had dreamed about for two years. We started with a Wild Water race on the River Washburn, near Leeds. I had been on some artificial and very easy white water at Cardington, near Bedford, in training, but the Washburn looked like the real thing. It was completely overwhelming and I refused to paddle it. In truth, I had talked myself out of racing there even before I saw the water. Paul was clearly disappointed in me, but it was one of his principles that people make their own decisions. Whatever I chose was down to me, and I would have to live with the consequences. It was the first time I had ever been given the opportunity to decide what I was doing with my own life. If Paul was disappointed with my decision it was nothing to the annoyance I felt with myself. I knew that I really did want to do it but I didn't think I was good enough. I went to the river with them because it was an integral part of a longer trip.

We then had a long drive down to Devon. We swapped boats here for plastic river kayaks and I was introduced to real white water for the first time. The River Dart was in flood. At the get-in the water was surging in a way that was new and intimidating. The trip Leader, Neil told us to get on and ferry glide across. My nerves threatened to get the better of me but, with some help from the others, my determination not to repeat the mistakes of the day before overcame them. My friend Carl took over my care.

"Ferry glide across the river."

"What's ferry gliding?"

"Don't you know what ferry gliding is?" Carl was amazed.

"No!"

"OK, just paddle to that tree." He pointed across the river. So that's what I did. It was easy. Carl followed me.

"What do I do now?"

"Paddle to that tree." I did that to and he came and joined me.

"That's ferry gliding."

"Oh, so I just paddle to trees?"

Carl was a little lost for words. I had successfully carried out the ferry glide, but I didn't know what I had done to do it. He could see that I was a natural, but I definitely didn't know what I was doing. I was going to need some work. I had a lot of trust in the paddlers with me, which was just as well because I had no idea what I was facing on the river. I had never really seen white water before, even though I was desperate to do it. I didn't understand the risks or the features.

About one hundred metres downstream from where we got in was a big weir, the first feature we would be paddling. All I could see was a line across the river where it suddenly vanished and, one by one, the group dropped over it, out of sight. Another girl was a little psyched out by it and I hung back with her, wondering what had happened to my friends that were disappearing. Carl came over and told us that we needed to make a decision. We could run the weir or walk around it. The other girl made her mind up instantly and got off the water. After a little indecision I followed her. As soon as I saw the weir from the river bank I knew that I had done the wrong thing. I felt I could easily have run it. I got back in the boat and was very annoyed with myself. I felt that I had given up too easily, a bit like I had done the previous day. I was determined that I wouldn't do it again. The next piece was easy, a short shingly rapid that gave me some confidence. Then we arrived at Schoolhouse Rapids.

"Why is it called Schoolhouse Rapids?" I asked Carl.

"You'll enjoy this," was his only reply. "Just smile and follow me."

"OK," I wasn't going to miss out, this time. "But where do I go?"

"Watch where I go and you go to wherever I'm paddling to. Just keep me in front. Just keep paddling."

We went over a little weir and paddled straight into some massive waves. We punched straight through them. I had a huge smile on my face. It was the most exciting thing I had ever done, a huge adrenaline rush. At the bottom of the rapid, apart from a "Yippee," I was speechless. It soon gave way to an excited chatter. When I looked around at the other beginners they looked a little white, some of them even looked a bit scared. I just thought it was amazing, the best roller coaster I had ever been on. As we got off the water someone said "Right, we're going to do it again."

"Let's go!" I said eagerly. It was a real let down when someone else explained that we were being teased and it was really lunchtime.

We were staying in a house in the Dart Country Park right near to where we had put in. While we were lunching the trip leaders went off to paddle the loop, a short and classic section of moderate white water that ended where we had put in. They came back beaming. The water was high and very exciting. This made a number of people in the room extremely nervous. I had no idea what they were on about, but I knew I wanted to go.

They brought us together and explained that, with the water running so high, they would not be taking everyone out on the afternoon trip. Only those they felt capable would be given an option to go. This being my first time on white water I assumed that I would be amongst those left behind. That was fair enough, I had had an amazing paddle already. I was wrong. I was given the choice to go. I asked whether they thought I would be able to do it.

"It's easy," said Carl, "just like this morning."

It wasn't. Eight of us went, Neil and Adrian, new coaches to me, together with my friends Carl and Paul looking after four of us newer ones. To begin with it felt quite flat, although fast. It was, as described, easy and like the morning's paddling. Then we arrived at the first big feature, a rapid called the Washing Machine.

"Why's it called the Washing Machine?" I asked, naively.

"Don't worry about that," Carl wasn't giving any more away in the afternoon than he had in the morning. "Just follow me."

It was an even bigger roller coaster. They kept the information simple "This one's just like a big slide;" "This one's just a lot of waves."

At Lover's Leap I was told to keep to the right, a harder line but reducing the chance of being pushed into a wall of rock at the bottom, and I followed it easily. The other beginners were taking swims, but I was just having fun. Then we reached Triple Falls, the most testing rapid in any conditions.

"On this one, you might get your face wet," Carl told me.

"Oh, ok." I was just looking forward to running it.

"You just have to paddle, but this time I'm going to go behind you."

"How will I know which way to go?"

"I'll shout directions."

So off I went, straight through a big haystack wave that combined both the first and second drops. As I came through I heard him shouting for me to paddle, and go right. I did and got another big face full of water. Then he shouted stop, and I was through. I stopped in an eddy with a big silly grin on my face. Everything was a huge exciting blur. It took a while to come down enough to notice that all the rest of the beginners in the group were swimming around me.

After that first run the water levels dropped. We had a couple more days there. We ran both the lower river where we had started and the loop several more times and I came away absolutely knowing that I had found my passion.

In the New Year Paul invited me on his "Frostbite Tour" to Scotland. A group of eighteen young people and coaches went up to run some serious white water. I was placed in hands of Carl and Adrian Slim, a coach I had paddled with on the Dart trip. Over the coming years I grew close to Adrian and his wife Jo, to the extent when their marriage broke up, years later, Adrian came to stay with me for a while. He was an intelligent and powerful paddler who eventually rose to take charge of coach education in East Anglia. He was very reassuring to paddle with, generally laughing whenever I swam, in a way that completely took away any fear.

I was partnered with a nice chap called Carlton. Once again there had been significant rain and the rivers were running very high. Our first river was the Spean. There were massive waves and, on the very first corner, I fell in and swam. For the first time I didn't have Carl to follow. I didn't know how to read a route through the river features and was making my own way. It was something of a wakeup call.

Carlton and I spent a lot of time in the water. I swam three times on that first day. I'm not sure how much was what I was learning, and how much was my fitness, but I quickly began to swim less. On the second day we did 12km of the Roy, I only swam twice and decided that I was doing better. On the third day I swam once. On the fourth day I didn't swim at all. Adrian was following us and he seemed to spend his days laughing and pulling me from rocks. I felt that I was the least experienced of all the paddlers on the trip, but I seemed to be learning quickest. I now understand that it is a mixture of physical and mental fitness. Your physical fitness counts for a fair bit but it is the ability of your mind to continually make decisions that makes a real difference in these testing conditions.

By the end of the trip I was happily paddling Grade IV water. I could pick my own routes and feel what the water was doing. I didn't necessarily understand everything but by the end of the week I was the most in control of my boat I had ever been and swimming the least. I had a real bug for white water and knew that I was going to be doing a lot more of it. Every moment I spent on it was amazing. The boat and I became one. When you walk you don't think about the shoes on your feet. By the end of that week my boat was just a part of me and I loved the freedom it gave me.

My new found freedom and passion was echoed in other areas, especially at school. From the moment I found paddling, I found myself and a way to communicate who I was. I stopped trying to be liked, which had only backfired on me. In return, life became easier, things like school exams, socialising all became a thing that just happened. They say there are some teachers that help shape your life, I was fortunate to have two who looked out for me especially before I found kayaking. In particular my maths teacher Janet Chambers was the first to believe in me. The natural affinity I have in a boat I also share in Maths. She really gave me confidence and in a similar way to Carl and Paul believing in my paddling ability made learning fun. Having these people have faith in me, helped me become truly happy rather than trying to appear happy. This gave me the strength I needed to get onto my first ever start line.

Two weeks later we came back to Scotland for my first Wild Water race. Once again the water was in flood but I had a lot more confidence. Paul and Carl showed me the best lines in the practice sessions but in the races I had to follow the line for myself. After our trips I had complete confidence in them and much more confidence in my own ability. I also knew that if I made a mistake the worst that would happen was a swim. My pride would be dented but I would be fine. Whilst I didn't win any of the races I did well enough to make an impression on a number of people there. Right from the start I was putting in good times and I felt a real sense of achievement. Paul was the National Junior Coach at the time and he invited me to a Junior GB training weekend at Holme Pierrepoint in Nottinghamshire. I wasn't part of the squad but the experience was terrific.

At the end of March there was another race on the Washburn. This was the Club Championships and the whole emphasis was on getting as many points as possible for the club. Every time I went out to do a run I was told that I was gaining points for the team (which was frequently the case). For me this took the pressure off. I could go out and do my best for the team. Unlike the Scottish rivers the Washburn was a narrow constant rapid, with overhanging trees to each side. For the practice runs Carl paddled close behind me, to help me if I got into trouble. He also shouted instructions. For the whole ten minutes of the run the only thing I heard him shout was "Paddle!" I think his voice took a real bashing that day. After that my motto became "Smile and Paddle."

To my surprise I won the race and was promoted to Division A, the top division. It was a bit of a shock and I didn't really understand what that meant at the time. A lot of girls had spent a long time working their way up the rankings and I had overleapt them in my second race. Paul was amused. Paul and Carl focussed on fun in their coaching and for them this was a validation of their methods. The fitness I had gained paddling long winters of race training had combined with their white water coaching and I was racing without even thinking about being competitive. If I had been aware of how difficult getting into Division A was my shaky self confidence might not have allowed me to do it.

That was the end of the racing season. Soon afterwards I passed my Level Two Coach's assessment. I was now a completely different paddler and person compared with the quiet girl who had gone in for her training. I had become much louder and more confident. I could easily control a group on the water and justify why I was doing what I was doing. I was developing my own ways of coaching and I was confident enough to justify it. Other coaches clearly respected the things I was doing. I built on it through the summer, coaching at an outdoor centre, and I had a fantastic time. It was my last full season at the Canoe Club in Essex. That autumn I went to

University an accomplished, happy paddler, coach and person.

# 8 THE EMERGING ATHLETE

By the time I went to University I had packed an incredible amount of paddling experience into a very short time. I had done quite a lot of coaching and paddled Grade V white water (the grading only goes up to six) I had tried surfing and got into the top division for Wild Water Racing. I had white water rescue training and I had set up lots of crazy safety work for Paul and Adrian running Grade V rivers in Scotland. I had more practical paddling experience than most paddlers and I thought it was the norm.

But if my confidence in a boat was high, my confidence socially still had a long way to go.

When I got to Loughborough University the first thing I did was join the canoe club. They asked me what I had done and I described it as 'a bit of white water.' They didn't explore that any further. My coaching qualification put me a good step ahead of any of them and I was quickly accepted and utilised coaching the other freshers. This was both good and bad. On the plus side I was immediately embedded in the club to the extent that many of my fellow first years thought I had been at the University for a while. This meant that I didn't get to bond with them in the way that they did with each other. I also fell into an unknown zone with the older students and didn't get invited to join them on the white water trips, after the freshers' trip that started the year off. In comparison to my coaches 'A bit of white water' was all I had done. Compared to most eighteen year olds I had done a huge amount.

Ironically the canoe club ran an advanced white water trip and I was not invited. My notion of advanced was Grade V rivers and I knew I was not good enough to do that with people I did not trust. However, I found out it was a Grade III, something that I was more than capable of. I was angry and cross and did not understand why I had not been asked. I kept myself from saying anything, still scared in many ways to speak out. It got to a point many weeks after the trip and my anger and intrigue spilled over, I asked why. I had fallen foul of my own miscommunication in describing my experience as 'a bit'. I had been in Paul and Carl's happy paddle bubble. I was not used to having to prove to people what I could do in a boat and showing off my skills on purpose. I was still very shy and reserved out of a boat and I believed my skills would show themselves. I was very wrong and had much to learn about life, as to when to 'show boat' and when to hold back.

Paddling wasn't my first priority at University. I was still competing with my sister and that meant I had to pursue a first class degree. I put my effort into working hard and meeting new friends. I was studying a joint degree of Sports Science and Maths. There was a small group of us taking the same mix of subjects. The first time that we sat quietly together between lectures one of the group decided to take the lead. Sally Jackson caught my attention immediately with her drawling Scunthorpe accent. It sounded outrageous to my southern ears. She is feisty, outgoing and outspoken. She started the group going with a series of questions: What A levels have you done? What results did you get? What sport do you do?

I was the first recipient of her questions and got off to a shaky start. It seemed I had similar grades to most of the group and then there was the sport question. I replied that I paddled kayaks. This drew slightly blank looks so I tried again.

"Almost any sport except Netball."

"Why not Netball?" I should have been warned by the way it was asked.

"Well, it's a bit poncey isn't it? I can't see the point in holding the ball and not running with it."

The temperature in the room dropped significantly. Sally then asked the other's the same questions. Sarah Blair, had been a national squad swimmer before injuries had cut her promising career short. She had replaced it with Hockey and Netball. Sharon Derbyshire was a county Netball player and very good all-rounder. Cara Holtam was an International Netball player. Sally owned up to netball, Football and Hockey. It took Cara a long time to forgive me but the rest of us quickly hit it off and I developed friendships with Sally and Sarah that are still strong to this day.

The work was much harder than I had expected, especially the maths, but our instant group was a huge help. Between lectures and tutorials we worked together on the problems we were set. In the evenings we shared our sports and enthusiasms. As night fell we would chat over the internal phone system, sharing our problems and troubles. We all helped each other through some very tough times that year and knew each other better than anyone else could. Towards the end of the first semester Sally asked Cara and I whether we knew each other.

Cara remembered the accidental slight I had given her at the start of the year, but it gave me the chance to apologise properly. She quickly became a part of our tight group and we were supporting her with her problems too. I had four really close friends, a better situation than I had ever had before.

I didn't paddle much white water that year. There was the problem of not being known as a white water paddler, but more importantly there was very little paddling available. That was the year that Foot and Mouth swept through the North West of England and many canoe clubs kept trips to an absolute minimum to avoid spreading the disease. The Canoe Club gave me an amazing social life. My status as a coach made me instantly socially acceptable. I could walk into a bar on campus and there would be people I had helped wanting to talk to me. Just wearing a canoe club hoody or t-shirt was enough to find me friends anywhere. I was a little overwhelmed with it.

I was also attracting interest from men for the first time, although I was so innocent I didn't realise it. On Valentine's Day I accepted and managed four invitations. I went for a drink with one young man, dinner with another, the cinema with a third and then played pool with a fourth. That evening my girlfriends asked me what I had been up to. When I told them they broke the news that all had probably been attempts at dates. I didn't know how to handle it. I broke off relations with all of them but two were harder to shake off. Mike began writing me love letters. John pursued me even harder so I relented and went out with him in the Summer Term.

That summer I had planned to travel to America to work at a summer camp. It was another important stage in my development. I went to Camp Weequahic in Pennsylvania without expectations and not knowing where it would lead me. We didn't get our assignments until we arrived. I was delighted to find that I had been assigned to the Waterfront Team but surprised to find that I was to teach Sailing. I had sailed a little with a school boyfriend, but had no qualifications.

The first week at camp, for the staff (or counsellors), is spent getting ready to receive the children. We work together to set it up, forming our teams and familiarising ourselves with our surroundings. The Canoeing Team were taken for a day's orientation on the River Delaware by a team of River Rangers. I had mentioned my paddling experience to the Head of Waterfront so I was invited to join them. It was quickly obvious that my skill levels were amongst the highest in the group. It seems that I impressed the Rangers too, because word got back to the camp before we did. On our return I was immediately informed that I had been transferred to the Canoe Team.

I loved my life in America. It seemed that foreign travel freed me from the restrictions of my childhood and let me become the person I had always needed to be. I became this hyper active happy huggy person. I could be open with my emotions and didn't have to be the strong young woman who my Mum and sister leaned on when they needed to. I don't think that I had ever laughed, smiled, cried or gone without sleep so much ever before. Americans are more open in telling you what they think, on the spot. I made quicker and deeper friendships than I had ever made before. Working in that tight knit environment meant that we became very close and could instinctively understand each other. I spent my days on the water and will never forget the experience of paddling with huge turtles. My evenings were spent looking after children.

With another counsellor I was responsible for a bunk room with eleven 9 and 10 year olds. Their age meant that they needed a lot of help with everyday things, but the compensation was that they loved to play and I could be very creative in coming up with entertaining ways of getting things done. I loved coming up with silly games like all brushing our teeth together. I also had to learn to apply discipline. I learned to give deadlines and countdown to them, getting everyone into a rush to finish in time. Telling them off, when they were naughty was a revelation. I really struggled to keep a straight face and would often have to walk away quickly afterwards. I realised that Mum had also had to do this to me when I was growing up. I used to think that it was a measure of how cross she was, but I now realise that she had to go to avoid laughing in front of me. Eventually the children caught me out and it seemed that they liked me even more for it. In many ways it was like having my own big family for a few weeks in another country.

When the camp ended I took the opportunity to travel. Around eleven of us climbed into a big white van that soon became known as Smelly Betty. We travelled in it for three weeks, going north into Canada via Niagara and coming back through Boston and down to Florida. We finished our tour in New York in early September. We stayed with the Head of Waterfront on Long Island. After a day exploring the area and relaxing on the beach we were due to head into the City for a day. We all slept in later than planned and took a leisurely breakfast before heading off. A telephone call prompted our host to turn the television on and we sat in stunned silence, watching as the first of the Twin Towers, part of the World Trade Centre group of buildings, burned and a second plane flew into the other Tower. The phone lines quickly jammed up as our hosts checked on friends and relations before all their communications overloaded and went down. It was a couple of hours before we even thought of telling our families that we weren't in the immediate vicinity of the disaster area.

The rest of our trip was difficult. Our hosts had known some of the people and Fire Fighters who went into the Twin Towers and needed space. We needed to go home but all the airports were closed. The airports opened briefly on the 13th and we went optimistically to the airport. Unfortunately it closed again almost at once. We spent the next, very uncomfortable, forty hours sleeping on the floor. The airport was a very unpleasant place to be. There were hysterical and irrational people everywhere. You could still see and smell the smoke from where the Twin Towers once stood. It was eerie and unnerving. The way I dealt with it was to detach myself from the situation and find the fun, where possible.

I had befriended a girl in the same situation as me and we worked together to keep our spirits up, playing I-spy, singing songs and trying to keep the people around us calm. We spent as much time as we could trying to get information and transfers onto a flight that might actually leave. Focusing on a solution seemed to me to be the best way to deal with the situation. Finally we were given seats on a flight. Nothing had left yet and there was no guarantee that the flight would actually take off. Eventually we were called and loaded into one of the first planes to fly out of Newark. The airline staff and the other passengers were obviously scared and we knew there were special agents on the flight. Each step was a small miracle. We finally took off and there was a lot of turbulence which made things worse. Eventually the pilot announced that we were over halfway and we were very relieved. At least if they closed the airspace now we would land in Europe. When we finally touched down the passengers gave the crew a huge round of applause. It didn't matter which airport this was, we were home.

That summer helped me a lot. I had worked out a lot about myself. It was probably the first time since I had seen the psychologist at school that I had really opened up about my feelings and emotions. I had a good idea of what I wanted from my life and I had lot more confidence. My paddling ability had been recognised in America, I had come through some very trying travelling situations and I knew myself better than I ever had. I ended my relationship with John and returned to University much more determined to get the best from the year ahead.

I threw myself into paddling. I helped coach the freshers and took part in their trips. In October we went to the Tryweryn in Wales, a grade 3-4 river that has become one of my favourites. I had been before, blindly following Adrian and Carl down the river. This time I was able to lead sections, even paddling backwards down rapids so that I could continue conversations. Mike was filling the gap in my life, offering trips and encouragement. I spent nearly every weekend in his company. It seemed to me that we just liked all the same things.

I made a decision that I wanted to take up Wild Water Racing again. I acquired an old carbon kevlar racing boat. It was a real speed machine, sleek and light but it was very battered before I restored it. One Saturday afternoon in November Mike drove me up to the Tees to enter a Wild Water race. By chance I met Paul there with his paddling partner, known to me only as Bartman. He was very pleased to see me racing again and gave me a lot of encouragement. It was very cold, there was ice forming on my paddle shaft as I practised. The water seemed to have it in for me, and I swam on every practise run. When my turn to race came I found my rhythm and both runs went perfectly. To my surprise I placed in the final results and came away with a trophy. More importantly, as it turned out, the GB Team Manager was there and he sought me out after my second race. He thought that my getting back into my boat every time I came out was gutsy and invited me down to a female training day in Bath a month later. I was very excited and jumped at the opportunity. Paul also invited me on the next Frostbite tour in Scotland with Chelmsford Canoe Club in February. Everything was falling into place.

I paddled in North Wales for both of the next two weekends, taking Freshers for their baptism of fire on the Dee Tour. I was happily leading groups doing classically demanding features like the Serpent's Tail and Town Falls in Llangollen. Where they were just trying to stay upright I was travelling backwards and chatting. This wasn't showing off. I just like chatting. I was still a little blasé. I didn't really think it was difficult. No-one had ever told me it was difficult so why would I expect it to be? It was just fun.

The following weekend I was back on the same river, racing in the British University Student Athletics Wild Water Race where I placed fourth. Things were going very well, without me having to try too hard. The training camp was a wonderful experience. Almost as soon as I arrived I met a kindred spirit. The prevailing atmosphere was very serious and focussed. Zoe Betteridge was a fabulous and committed paddler, but she was every bit as crazy as me. We were both told off for singing on the river instead of putting every ounce of breath to use driving our boats forward. We wanted to do well, but it was also important to enjoy ourselves. We were to see a lot of each other over the next couple of years.

In February I took off to Scotland for a week with my old friends on my second Frostbite Tour. It was wonderful to be paddling with them. All the big water trips I had done were with Paul, Adrian and Carl. I trusted them completely, they knew what they were doing and must surely know my limitations. If any one of them said "Follow me" I would do so without hesitation. Paul would ask me whether I thought I could make a line and if I said "yes" he would send me off. In the two years since we had last been together I had gone from being one of the weakest paddlers in the group to one of the strongest. I was strong and confident and wanted to see just where my limits were. The weather had been very wet and the rivers were ready to help me with the task. In a week of stupendous paddling some moments really stand out.

Our first river was the Spean. The level is controlled by a dam, automatically releasing water as it maintains the level of the loch above. Guide books talk about one, two or, rarely, three pipes releasing water into the river. When we arrived at the get in five of the six pipes were running. Getting onto the river was like being in a monsoon with the spray from the pipes and some of the group were looking very nervous. As I prepared to let go of the bank we heard a loud ticking noise, followed by an almighty boom as the final pipe opened and let even more water through. It was one of the biggest bits of water I have ever paddled. I was paddling with Bartman and found that I was close to my limit. The stoppers were as big as houses, missing the line and dropping into one would be a disaster. I found that the best way to cope with the sheer volume of water was to turn around and paddle up stream, ferry gliding to the right bit of river before each drop. It was a very intense experience, and even though there was nowhere to stop and think, my subconscious knew what to do. I settled into the paddling and the two mile stretch of river flew by. At the end many of the group seemed quite stunned. I was embracing it.

The River Orchy is a classic run. We scouted out Eas a Chataidh, a grade five fall over a sheer drop with a complicated exit line.

"Where do you think the line is?" Paul asked.

"I think it's about there."

"Ok, are you comfortable with it?"

"Yeah, I am."

"Ok off you go. I'll bag you, but you have to be prepared to bag me." Throwlines or bags are buoyant bags filled with floating line and are the first recourse for rescue in most white water situations.

We both ran the fall successfully. I looked to Carl to see if he was going, but he shook his head. It was only then that he told me it was grade five. He showed me where it could have gone wrong and what might have happened if I'd strayed into any of those features.

"Didn't you think about it? He asked.

"No," I replied, "I wasn't going to go near either of them. I knew there were risks, but they never seemed to affect me.

We did a speed run on the River Etive. Two years before we had paddled this memorable river. It is an adrenaline junkie's paradise with lots of waterfalls and big drops into pools. I took a swim on the way down, but we still managed to complete it in 27 minutes. This is one of my treasured paddling moments and one I have happily relived in my dreams.

One incident began to awaken a fear response. We had river racer boats with us and chose to run the River Arkaig. We had run it a couple of days before. Today it was higher and so was my confidence. Paul and Bartman were faffing around, getting ready in their tandem boat and I ran out of patience. "I'll catch you at the bottom!" I shouted and set off without them. The river was massive. I spent half of the run just trying to keep my tippy racing boat upright. I reached a rapid that turned out to be grade five in that water level and the water just got the better of me. I capsized and I couldn't roll back up. I knew I was on my own so I had to rescue myself. I kept trying, getting my head out of the water to breathe on each attempt but not quite managing the full roll. I stayed in the boat until I managed to spin it around and up just above a big drop into a raging hole; my heart pounding nineteen to the dozen, and the adrenaline flowing. I was in an eddy against an Island in the centre of the stream. I looked at my options and thought a rude word. The only real solution was to run the drop or wait for rescue. I knew it wouldn't end well but I made my decision.

I broke my boat out into the flow, managed to turn it around for one paddle stroke and then I dropped into the hole. Without the speed I needed to push through I stopped dead and was munched. I went straight over. My paddle was taken from me, I came up for air and then the water sucked me right out of the boat, releasing the spray deck, breaking two thigh bars and the foot rests on the way. It was one of the most unpleasant swims I have ever had. I was pulled down into the depths of the undercurrents. I remember thinking "How am I going to get back up?" My feet eventually touched a rock and I pushed off it, remembering to swim as hard as I could. I was completely disorientated. I reached the surface after being under for at least thirty seconds. When I finally came back up I was clear of the hole and was gasping for air but had no real idea of what had happened. I was in auto pilot and I managed to grab my boat and swam into a big eddy on the right. I was up and walking, still panting when Paul and Bartman arrived, carrying their boat.

"Cool!" Bartman said.

"I think I handrolled," I said, my talent for avoiding the seriousness of a situation at full capacity still.

"I know, how cool was that?"

"I think I lost my paddle, can you look for it?"

"Yeah, yeah, we'll try to get it for you."

"How come you didn't do it?"

"Well, we looked at it and thought: Nah. It was stupidly big."

Paul and I have talked about it since and he told me that there was no way they were going to risk running it. I had just gone for it without thinking too much. After that I began thinking twice and wasn't quite so gung ho. I had to walk out with what was left of my bout. I had swollen knees from the sucking out and cuts and bruises all over the place. I hobbled for the next two weeks and my knees weren't right for a long while. For all that, main annoyance from it was that I couldn't ride my bike to lectures for a while as it was difficult to bend my knees. It didn't stop me getting back on the water but it did make me a bit more cautious. In a river racer you have to be absolutely sure about where you are going to paddle. If you have the slightest feeling that you might fall in somewhere you are almost guaranteed to swim. After that I went through a phase of doing more swimming, in my river racer, but I always got back in.

Back at University I produced the photos at a canoe club social. They were passed round to a lot of admiring noises. Then I heard one of the better paddlers ask "Who is that paddling?"

"It's Gilly."

"Oh, I didn't think she could paddle white water?"

"What do you mean?" I had to ask.

"Well, what have you paddled?"

I gave them a list.

"No, you can't have done."

"Well," I said, "That's the pictures."

"Oh. How much white water have you done?"

"I've only done a bit," I said.

"Hang on a minute," he said, "You're a competent Grade IV paddler and you've clearly done some Grade V in the pictures. Why do you think that's only a bit?"

"Well, in comparison to some of the guys I paddle with that is only a bit."

The penny dropped for both of us. We both knew that I had done more than most people. Not only was I very comfortable on grade four moving water, I could lead people down grade four. Sadly it was too late. My focus now was Wild Water Racing and for the first time I was training hard with a goal in sight. Zoe had been in touch about the Student World Championships and we both had a very good chance of being selected.

Throughout March and April I spent almost every weekend away at races in Scotland, Wales and the North of England. I was consistently placing in the top five, but wasn't sure whether this was going to be good enough. At the end of March we went to the Tryweryn for a division B race, with the main priority being to learn the river. The Tryweryn is a very difficult river to read and the selection race would be held there soon. Paul dealt with my nerves by paddling alongside and splashing us, reminding us that, as serious a task as it was, it should also be fun. He led us down a couple of times and then Zoe and I teamed up for the first time and paddled it together. We found that one corner looked a lot like another and we had a constant conversation about the line.

"I think it's left here."

"Are you sure?"

"Yes. Er, I think it is?"

"How confident are you?"

"Ninety nine percent"

"Too late now." We were in the rapid.

"Yep. A hundred percent sure now."

We took a long time on that run but we never forgot the lines again. Paul was monitoring our progress, popping up in numerous places once pretending to be a fisherman. He said that he had never heard so much talking on a run, and that it was like watching a couple of gossiping mothers trying to paddle a river. He was no longer coaching the Junior Team so he was free to run us a mini training camp the following weekend and we returned to the Tryweryn a fortnight later for the selections.

Paddling a Wild Water Racing boat is all about getting the right line down a rapid, and then doing it at the fastest speed possible. It requires instant decisions and you have to be one hundred percent confident in that decision. If there is the slightest thought that you might swim then you certainly will. After my experience on the River Arkaig in February I seemed to be doing a lot more swimming in races. Whether it was my experience in that big stopper or the extra pressure I was putting myself under I will never know. The weekend of the selection race was no exception. I swam six times at Miss Davies Bridge and six more times at Chapel Falls. Every time I got back in. At least on the race run I managed to complete the course without swimming. The coaches and race selectors didn't seem to mind. I loved the white water so much that where others were giving up I would just keep trying until Carl or Paul told me to try it again later. I still had a lot to learn. In the end my persistence won them over and my place in the Student World Championships in Krakow was secure.

I have found many parallels to life in river racing. You have to take constant decisions, choosing routes and committing to them. Sometimes you can change your path but every choice has a consequence and you will have to take that, whether it is good or bad. People can advise you, show you the way to go, advise you on the right line, but when it comes down to it, and you are there on the river, the route you want is not always the one you end up taking. It takes a certain level of self belief to lead yourself down a white water river. As I ran more rivers I learned from the experience and became more confident, but there is a fine line. Overconfidence can lead to disaster.

The selections were the last race of the season for me. At University I was playing canoe polo and helped Mike to organise the BUSA Canoe Polo Tournament. Our team included Fiona Pennie, later an Olympic slalom paddler and Sharon Derbyshire from my degree course. Sharon was also planning to spend the summer working in the American Camp system and we spent many happy hours talking about it. My summer plans were simple. A lot of fitness work to make sure I would do well in Krakow and prove to the selectors I was a serious competitor and a return to Camp Weequahic. Everything was going very well.

# 9 ONE STEP TOO FAR

The summer of 2002 was a real turning point in my life. From starting my A levels to going to Uni I had cruised through. Everything seemed to go my way. I had good friends, I was doing well in a sport that I loved, and I was on track academically. The biggest problem I had was that there were people in Wild Water Racing who thought I didn't take my training seriously. I intended to train hard that summer and go home the fittest mentally and physically I had ever been. Nothing could possibly go wrong.

I flew out to America for my second stint at Camp Weequahic. High expectations are a dangerous thing, but it exceeded them. I was reacquainted with children I had met the year before who were delighted to see me again, and not only because I remembered their names. This time there was no doubt about it, I was to work on the waterfront again. I didn't have a bunk of children to care for because of the amount of time I would spend on trips. It was odd not to have that responsibility at first, but it freed a lot of time for fitness training. I found a training partner in another British Counsellor, Pete. Together we would get up early in the mornings to swim and run before the rest of the camp woke up. It was brilliant for me. We had a lot in common and we had strengths that complimented each other. We were able to help and push each other with our weaknesses.

Pete also worked on the waterfront so we spent a lot of time together, putting the world to rights. I became very fit, my body changed shape as I put on muscle. It even drew positive comments from other counsellors. I felt strong both inside and out and I'm sure I bounced everywhere rather than walk. I had never had so much energy and drive. I was busy every minute of the day and had become an important part of the canoe team. One counsellor shocked me when she comforted a nervous child by referring to me as a professional canoeist. I was allowed to make changes to the way things were done and I felt very much that I was a respected part of the team. I couldn't have been happier.

Outside the camp things were moving on to. I was in regular contact with Zoe, putting together our arrangements for the trip to Poland. I was planning to travel after camp, and Mike was going to fly out to join me. Then I received a post card from Sharon, the university friend I had discussed camps with. She was in the same State at an all girl camp. I looked at maps and asked the older counsellors and realised that I could get there and back in a day. Pete and I made it our mission to go and surprise her on one of our five days off. Even with a map it wasn't easy to find and we were about to give up when we eventually found it. Sharon was just as busy as me, but the camp staff were helpful and gave her some time off. Pete had to stay in reception while another counsellor led me to the bunkhouse where they had blindfolded her to add to the surprise. Sharon confused until, for some strange reason she recognised my feet and leapt at me in utter shock. It was a lovely moment for us both, thousands of miles from home.

In the last couple of weeks I made a new and lasting

friend. Samantha Vigil was having trouble with discipline
in her bunkhouse. I knew her reasonably well from
working together on a couple of trips. At twenty we don't
always find discipline with children easy. She had been
struggling with a particularly difficult group of girls. By
the end of the camp things were so bad that none of the
counsellors wanted to take this bunkhouse on. I was asked
to help by the head counsellor and I moved into the bunk.
My experience from the previous year paid off as I made it
clear to the girls that nothing they could do would work on
me and followed it through. The bunk settled down and
Sam and I became very close friends in the last weeks of
camp. She made me an offer I was quick to include in my
travelling plans – she lived in Albuquerque, New Mexico,
close to one of the places I desperately wanted to visit: the
Grand Canyon. It was only 400 miles away. Staying with
Sam meant we could visit it together.

The long summer camp came to its eventual end and I
reluctantly left it. Pete had offered me a lift down to Texas
as part of his travelling plans which I had happily accepted.
It wasn't a good move. I had realised rather late that he
had interpreted our closeness as a romantic interest.
Fortunately Mike was coming to join us for the road trip
which would give us a distraction. We picked Mike up
from a nearby town and there was immediate tension
between the two. I hadn't really thought about it, but it
was clear that both boys were vying for my attention. In
my long friendship with Mike he had offered to be more
than friends but I didn't feel it and we had never taken our
friendship further. He had sent letters to America the
previous year but I thought nothing of it. Subsequently I
reread them and suspect they were love letters. In the
enclosed space of Pete's truck you could almost see them
starting to lock antlers. The truth was that I didn't want a
relationship with either of them: there was someone who
was back in England that I was much more interested in.
The journey was beautiful but awkward silences were more

common than excited chatter as we travelled south and the green mountains gave way to buff deserts. The accents grew thicker, slower and stranger as the people got friendlier.

We parted in Dallas, Texas. It was a relief to be out of the tension in the truck. We had been travelling for twenty two hours without a break. Mike and I had only the loosest of travelling plans. I find this kind of travel the most exciting. The only thing we were sure of was that we would visit Sam in Albuquerque. We took an overnight Greyhound Bus over the State Border to Portales, New Mexico, a tiny town in the middle of nowhere. On the bus Mike confessed to me that he had lost his wallet. I had thought he was an experienced traveller, but he wasn't as travel wise as I thought. He still had his important documents and most of his cash. It was frustrating to have lost his credit cards and to have to sort out cancelling his documents.

We arrived to heavy rain at five in the morning. We took refuge in a donut restaurant to watch the downpour and gather ourselves. Through the window we could see a full sized plane that appeared to be parked in the middle of the road. We puzzled over it while the rain fell and created a large puddle around it. We entertained ourselves speculating on why the plane was there and watching cars negotiating the puddle. Eventually one of them stopped in the middle and was stuck. Mike and I looked at each other then walked outside and pushed. We were both wearing sandals and were already soaked through, a condition canoeists are thoroughly used to, so we thought nothing of it. The rest of the restaurant patrons were very impressed by our act of kindness. It turned us into small town local celebrities. Everyone seemed to know who we were and we were overwhelmed with offers that ranged from free donuts to lifts to wherever we wanted. We made a decision to splash out on a motel for the night (and most of that day) to catch up with sleep and get ourselves into a better state for the journey. Our local celebrity status was good enough to get us a lift from a local sheriff to his favourite restaurant for a meal that evening and we were in a much better state the next day when Sam came to pick us up.

In Albuquerque we joined Sam and her roommate, Jen in their new apartment. We also met Jen's twin sister, Kim, who lived in the next door complex. They are a tight team who have been friends since childhood. I hadn't met the twins before but we took to each other straight away. Mike was quieter but they loved his Welsh accent. Jen had moved into it a couple of days before, prior to the new year starting at Albuquerque State University. There was no furniture yet and the first time Jen saw us was when we carried a bookcase into the apartment with Sam's Dad. That evening we shared a big bowl of pasta on the floor. It was delicious and eaten with a great deal of giggling. School term having just started, Sam, and the twins were going to be busy signing up for classes and heavy workloads. Mike and I had plans anyway.

Albuquerque sits on a high plain across the Rio Grande River. To the east, the Sandia Mountains tower over the town. Sandia is Spanish for Watermelon and in the right light the mountains are a beautiful mix of green and pink rock. We planned a couple of small walks in the Sandias to pass the time until the weekend and our trip to the Grand Canyon. On the first day we followed a trail to the top. It only took us four hours but we learned a valuable lesson about walking in heat. Somewhere on the way back I became aware that Mike wasn't drinking properly. We were at 6,000 feet in a desert climate and that evening he was quite ill. I was very cross and disappointed in him. Even worse for the first time I was embarrassed by him. I had told him he needed to drink and he hadn't. I didn't want to have to look after him in the way I did the camp kids. It was the first time we had really argued. The next day we took a rest.

We had made our Grand Canyon plans before we left camp. We were going with Sam and Annamarie, another Weequahic Counsellor who also lived locally. On Friday we drove the four hundred miles to the campsite. Sam and Annamarie were less athletic than Mike and I so our plans for the days diverged a little. On Saturday they did their sightseeing at the top, with the aid of a snooze and an Ice Cream. Mike and I started down a path at two o'clock in the afternoon. It was really hot and like an oven as we hiked down into the Canyon. After our experience on Sandia I was paranoid about dehydration. I drank at every opportunity, every one and a half miles on the Bright Angel Trail there was a water tap. I bugged Mike all the time to make sure he drank to. At the three mile rest point, Mike knew that I wanted to go further but he was slowing me down. As you looked from the top of the South Rim, you could see Plateau Point and Indian Head campground. I was desperate to get to one of them. Being in the Canyon was infectious and I just wanted to see more and more of it. I had to hold myself back even though Mike offered to let me go on alone. We had both travelled a long way for this and I wanted to do it together or not at all. We had a long chat, whilst sitting on a log and took in the scenery. This place just fascinated me and I felt very close to nature and was in awe of this magnificent place. We then turned back to go up the steep trail to join up with Annamarie and Sam. We all took a bus to the viewpoints together before heading back to the campsite and driving home early the next day. I loved the Grand Canyon and swore that one day I would come back and walk the whole way down to the river.

On our return we had three days before we were due to fly out to spend our last few days in New York exploring Central Park. This was something that the previous year's disaster had prevented me from doing. We planned to spend them camping and walking in the Jemez Mountains, about an hour and a half's drive away. Sam was to drive us and we set off with high hopes, but as we approached them we could see plumes of smoke above the trees. As we got closer the smoke cloud grew. Traffic coming in the opposite direction began to increase rapidly. Eventually it was clear that the area had been hit by forest fires and we reluctantly turned back, passing fire trucks racing in the other direction.

We had two days left to decide what to do with. My body and mental state were still on a camp timetable. I was time oriented and organised everything with songs and activities whenever we stopped. I was watching everyone carefully for behaviour changes, reminding them to drink and eat. This was annoying Mike. It wasn't behaviour he was used to. I was more tired than I was trying to let on after the business of camp, which meant our tempers flared more easily. I was ready to rest and would have been happy to spend my time relaxing and chatting with my new friends. My needs for the travelling had changed. I had done enough outside adventures and I was ready to take some downtime. The Grand Canyon had left me feeling quite calm and happy with myself. I wanted to take stock of where I was and enjoy my surroundings. Nothing was quite going to plan and I would have been happy to stay put but Mike had come for an adventure at my invitation. Having lost our camping trip together we needed to find something else to do.

On the Tuesday we borrowed Sam's car and took ourselves off for a walk in a National Park a few miles away. There were supposed to be Petroglyphs on the walls, a local attraction. We took a packed lunch and drove out to the National Park in silence. Our nonsense conversations seemed to be at an end. I tried a number of open questions to get him talking. Eventually he told me about his summer in a Welsh outdoor centre but it still didn't flow properly. The Petroglyphs turned out to be some uninspiring (I apologise to any petroglyphologists reading this) rock markings. This finally made us laugh.

We didn't understand why they were held in such high regard but we made a game of finding them and entertained ourselves interpreting them in our own idiosyncratic way. It broke the ice a little and our day improved. An information board in the car park told us that there was a dormant volcano nearby. This was more our kind of place so we set off to find two dusty dark brown rocky mounds behind a picnic area.

The view was amazing, with Albuquerque sitting in its plain, surrounded by mountains. We raced each other to the top. Sitting high on the slope we watched planes carrying water in the direction of the Jemez Mountains and talked things through. There was a lot of air to clear. Mike had told me that he wanted a closer relationship and I tried to let him down as gently as I could. We had done this once before. Back in March he had asked me out and I had turned him down. I just didn't see him that way. We had so much in common that we were almost soul mates, but there was no romantic spark, at least on my side. I saw him as something more like a big brother. I really valued his friendship and wanted that to continue and I thought it had. Sadly the girls had pointed out to me that his body language and behaviour said differently. I looked again and realised that it was true. There was a rising tension between us that we had to sort out. Small things had been irritating us both and if we were not to waste the rest of our holiday we needed to agree how to behave with each other. It took time but I felt that we succeeded, and had time to speculate about the forest fire in the distance. It occurred to me that if we had set off sooner the day before we might have been stuck there. Neither of us had phones and it would have been difficult to get back in touch with Sam to get away. We thought it was a lucky escape.

Afterwards we let off steam, heading for a large Wal-Mart and playing with the toys like a pair of big kids. This was more like our normal relationship. We made plans for the following day; I had been in charge of everything so far so Mike was to take the lead. He suggested that we go to see the sunset from the top of the Sandia Mountain. The colours in Albuquerque are gorgeous and they are reputed to be even better from the top of the mountain that overlooks the town. We planned a walk that was strenuous by local standards, but Mike had spent his summer leading children in the Mountains of Wales and I saw it as altitude training for my fitness. If it was too much then we had a fallback option: to come down on the Tram, a big cable car that takes tourists to the top. That evening we went to a local hotel and played in the swimming pool with Sam, Kim and Jen. They also took us to a Dunkin Donuts drive through. I don't think it was something in the food but we had some strange conversations. We spent a couple of hours messing about and things felt normal again.

We woke later than usual the next morning. I wasn't my usual merry self so I left the preparations to Mike, who was already up and making food for the trip, while I checked my emails. There was news from lots of friends and a message from Zoe with the final timetable for our trip to Poland. I replied to them all with my news of hiking and watching the sunset. In a better mood I wrote some postcards for Sam to post for us. It completely restored my good humour and I was ready to join in again. Helping to pack the lunch into our day bag, I was surprised to see clouds outside. These were the first clouds we had seen since we arrived and they made me feel tired. If I had been on my own I would have taken a rest day, but there was a momentum and I was determined to enjoy our walk.

I wore shorts and a sleeveless T-shirt for the walk. We weren't expecting bad weather. On my feet I wore sandals. I've been criticised for this choice but I had spent the whole summer running, walking and climbing in them without trouble. I had already worn them for walking up the Sandia Mountain, on the volcano and part way down the Grand Canyon. I was sure that they were up to the terrain. Mike had a blister from walking in sandals at the Canyon so he wore his boots.

Sam dropped us in the pre-arranged car park and we set off for the hillside. I took the first turn with the rucksack. It was quite heavy. We had a lot of water because we didn't expect to find any more on the desert hillside. We had learned the lesson of Mike's dehydration on a previous walk on the Sandia Mountain Range. We set off at good pace and I was soon trailing. Partly this was so that we didn't have to talk – our conversation of the day before still cast a shadow over our ease with each other; partly because Mike was setting a fast pace. I think he was on a mission to prove that hills were his territory. I didn't call him back because I didn't want him to think I was struggling with the pack. I also had to prove that I wasn't still "Camp Gilly" who needed to be in constant charge of what was happening.

The day was overcast but still warm, the terrain was much harder than I had expected; constantly up and down and changing direction. It was hard to tell whether we were on the right route or not. Without the map I simply followed, our constraint keeping me from asking whether we were going the right way. I wasn't taking a real interest in my surroundings. I had my head down and looked at my feet, the time had come to get it over with and go home to Britain. I was already living in the future. I was thinking of things to come: a white water safety and rescue course I had booked at Plas y Brenin which promised to be a real adventure, the two day drive to Poland with my paddling buddies. I couldn't wait to get back into my white water boat. It made me under enthusiastic about the day when we spoke in a way that must have been very transparent. The Gilly who went up the mountain on the 28th August 2002 was a quiet Gilly, not the woman I had become.

I'm sure Mike knew that I didn't want to be there. I don't know how that affected him, or whether it contributed to the events later that day. We had stopped talking. I trailed further and further behind, dwelling on the distance between us, the lack of happy conversation and the way he was on a mission. I went through a whole variety of emotions; from being angry, to frustrated, to upset, to complete puzzlement as to what I was doing and why I was out walking. I walked along muttering to myself, keeping out of earshot of Mike. The tension between us was back. Perhaps he needed time to sort out his feelings. He looked around and stopped every so often, but took off as soon as I reached him. This fuelled my internal annoyance at the situation. The rucksack began to wear me down but I held on to it for as long as I could. I wasn't having fun. I may have been a bit off colour, but it was his day and our friendship needed it to go well. I needed to change my attitude to being more positive and to find the fun in what we were doing. However, the path got rougher and rougher. I now know that we were already off the path. When I went back two years later I could see that it was fairly easy to go wrong. We had taken a route up the wrong gully. If we had paused and checked both directions we would have seen a signpost around the next corner, but neither of us saw it.

The rock on the Sandia Mountain is very sandy and my sandals began to slip. The ground grew steadily tougher and steeper as we climbed. We began to have to scramble over boulders. This was much harder than we had expected, but we could do it. We didn't question it any more than that. My head was down and I was just following. At the same time I was annoyed with myself. I was making hard work of it in a way that was uncharacteristic for me. I tried to distract myself, reminding myself that it was like climbing the rocks at the sea front, when I went looking for rock pools. As a child I would bound up those and other hilly climbs like a mountain goat.

At about 2 or 3 o'clock in the afternoon we were definitely not on a path. We took a break and the chance to eat. I sat on a rock and looked down at Albuquerque. The plain spreads for miles. I took a picture on my camera for posterity. I could see small dust storms and low lying clouds obscuring the blue skies, orangey landscape and buildings I had got used to. It all oppressed me. It was clear that we still had a long way to go and we needed to change our plans. We decided that we would press on, but take the Tram back down. Mike took the backpack when we set off again, moving up as quickly as we could.

There was no path at all now. I began to get a nasty feeling in the pit of my stomach. I wasn't climbing well and everything seemed to be more difficult than it should be. Mike was in front and going faster than me so I had to work hard to stay with him. We eventually reached some kind of plateau and stopped for another drink. I remember running around it, making aeroplane noises to try to bring some fun back into the day. Mike just laughed at me as I ran about. For me it was a release of my pent up emotions and was my way of relaxing. After that, my body didn't seem to ache as much and I felt I had much more energy back in my system. The steepness of the terrain continued but was not quite so severe and we climbed on upwards towards the top of the mountain. The strained air between Mike and I had lifted and we were finally talking again, making up stories about who could live here, high on the mountain. We were enjoying each other's company in the way we always had, playing imagination games and talking nonsense. It looked as if we were back on the path and the walking was easier. My stomach eased up on me and I put my sandals back on. We were getting, we thought, quite near to the top. We had a choice between going left to a ridge or following the tree line to the right. I thought left was the more likely option but Mike was the more experienced walker of the two of us. I trusted his experience in the same way that I did Paul or Carl when paddling. So I backed his decision to go right. I found out later that left would have been a better decision.

We gained height along the tree line quite quickly as the slope below steepened, making me feel very exposed. Passing the tree line we reached what looked like a group of huge boulders, stacked on top of each other. We were going to have to climb. The fear of falling came back to me together with the unsettled stomach. I was quite anxious; we had no ropes or safety equipment and I have never been a climber. Before this day I had been on a climbing wall once. I blindly continued to follow Mike, talking to myself to keep calm and reiterating that I trusted him. I very quickly began losing control and was spiralling into a weak mental state. I lost my ability to make my own decisions and assess the risk I was running, to the point where if I was asked to put my head into a hot oven, I would have done. I needed separate instructions as to where to place each hand and foot and could not multi task. I could move my hand and then had to be told again where to place my foot. For speed and reassurance, Mike began to shove me up. I kept myself so close to the rock surface that my tummy was scraping against the dirt. Some of the boulders on their own I could have coped with in a normal situation, but the continuous nature of them, the exposure and the height we had gained escalated the difficulty. Mike tried to help me by letting me stand on his knee or he would hold my foot from below. At the top of each I felt I had achieved something, but I had no idea how I was doing it. On top of the third I began to cry. I felt as if I was in a nightmare. To avoid falling I had to stay very close to each boulder. I could feel the grit on my cheeks, mingling with my tears and sweat. To this day, I can still taste and feel the grit inbetween my teeth and the roughness of the rocks on my cheek and left shoulder. I had never been that scared in my life before and had never been in a situation where I truly feared for my life. For his part Mike was unfailingly encouraging. I could only apologise for being a mess.

There was a well of tension building up in me. I knew I should stop this; that I couldn't keep going up, but I didn't have the courage to say it. My internal voice was quietly saying 'say No', 'say Stop', but I didn't. At the fourth big boulder I was shaking and freezing up. The exposure took away my sense of balance. It felt as if I had gone over the top of a ride, throwing my stomach into the air in a way from which it could not come down again. My centre of gravity was raised, making me feel unstable and weak. My head was full of images of people falling; sometimes Mike, sometimes me. Every one of my instincts was telling me that we had to stop, but I stayed quiet. My internal voice was getting slowly louder and louder. I was, by now, an experienced outdoors woman and I knew we were in trouble. However strong Mike might be on the mountain I was completely beyond my abilities. Since that day I have wrestled with why I didn't say no earlier and have been unable to explain it. I was embarrassed and ashamed at the lack of courage I had and time has only lessened some of those feelings. Initially being off the path wasn't a problem. I had faith in Mike's judgement. My paddling experience had been with amazing companions that I had trusted absolutely and I had the same faith in Mike on a mountain. He had a Mountain Leader's certificate and had been on mountains all over Britain and even in Chile.

I finally crawled onto the top of the fourth boulder, sobbing. Somehow Mike was there before me, picking me up, encouraging me on. It was flat again for a short while before we reached a fifth boulder. Every instinct within me was screaming for us to stop. I finally said something.

"We need to stop. I can't do this."

"Come on, come on. You're doing really well."

"Mike, I'm really scared." My voice was shaky.

"You're doing fine. There's no problem. I know what we're doing."

"I'm out of my depth. I can't climb." I tried again to explain how nervous I was to Mike.

"You're doing brilliantly well."

Whatever I said, he came back with an encouraging comment and he won me over. Even though I was struggling he seemed to be able to bounce up everything, so it must have been ok.

At the sixth boulder I was completely out of control. I couldn't focus for the tears. I was sobbing and couldn't stop. I looked down at him as he held my left foot and pushed me up. I told him that this had to be the last one. I couldn't keep putting myself through this. Mike finally agreed with me. As my head appeared over the top of the boulder and I clutched for something to pull the rest of me up. I didn't want to look ahead of me and secretly wanted that to be the last thing I pulled myself up. So I didn't dare look until both feet were firmly on the ground. When they were I looked up from my feet. My heart sank and I collapsed onto my knees. In front of us was some heavy vegetation, prickly cacti and yet another huge boulder to climb. This one was far bigger than the last. I was exhausted and couldn't do it. I must have cried for a good five minutes before I could talk or even lift my head up. I could see that it was getting to him too. He promised me that he would find us a way off and left me for a while to scout for a way down. I didn't move for a long time. It took a lot of energy just to gather myself together. I was a hysterical mess. Trying to draw a continuous breath in through my nose was interrupted by my body shuddering. I was making whimpering noises. After a while I shifted my breathing to my mouth and I was able to take in my surroundings once more. It was like a switch had been turned on: I suddenly realised that Mike knew he was out of his depth too. I knew that I had to make a huge effort to help him and we needed to work as a team. Our instincts had put us in very different places: mine was to stop; his had been to keep going, keeping me moving up the mountain to try to get out of it. It's very hard to know who was right.

He came back with good news.

"I've found a way down. I've scouted it out. I can see the Cable Car and it's easier going."

"I can't climb up any more." I was adamant about that.

"It's ok. It's fine. It's downhill all the way. We can get to where the Cable Car is and there will be a service road for the Pylons. We'll be able to follow that down." That sounded sensible to me.

"Have you checked all the options?" I wanted us to make a proper decision.

"Yes, it's fine. I've been all over the place. I've checked it." As far as I could see he had thrown off the panic my upset state had put him into. The break in our pace had put him back in control and he was radiating confidence. I got up off my knees and followed him. Subsequently I found that there was a better option. He hadn't checked properly. When I went back seven years later I found that if he had checked more ways we could have been back on the Path in less than a hundred yards. There was even a signpost, just out of sight of where we had stopped. The summit ridge was right behind it.

Round the corner of the boulder the gully began to run downhill, through a thicket of prickly bushes. The relief I felt was immediate. The ground sloped steeply and was bringing us down quite quickly. We slid on our bottoms, laughing about explaining the scratches later. Before long we came upon a tree across our route. We had to climb over it. My nervousness returned immediately: the slope was steep enough that losing grip of the tree on the other side could lead to a nasty fall. Mike went back into reassurance mode. He climbed back to where I was frozen still and offered me his hand to help guide me. It worked better this time. We made it over the tree and the dread of something bad happening left me. Mike was good at descending and once again was away ahead of me, finding the route and making more headway. We were in a steep sided gully, about ten metres wide, descending at an angle of about thirty degrees from the vertical. We couldn't zigzag much, but I could traverse at times, mostly to my right. It wasn't slippery, but you had to constantly find your way between the bushes. This meant that I didn't notice it immediately, but we were losing height very quickly. Every foot made me feel better. Then I came around a bush and suddenly caught Mike up. He had stopped.

"Where do we go then, Mike?" I said it in quite a cheery tone which showed how my temperament had changed from only a short time ago.

"There's bad news."

"What's that?" My heart sank. What else was going to be thrown at us to contend with?

"Well, this gully sort of stops here. Don't go near the edge!"

"I don't want to go near the edge. Where do we go?" I was quite pragmatic with my response and the words and question came almost automatically. I could see the options. I didn't like them so I needed to hear him say it.

"These are the choices: straight down, straight up this rock face or we can go back to where we came from." I hadn't thought that my heart could sink any lower than it already was. I looked up ahead at the rock face. I already knew what was behind me.

"I need to have a look." My instinct was to try to continue down. That would bring us closer to home and away from this horrible situation. I moved forward closer to the edge to look at the last option.

"Don't go too close, I don't want you to fall over it."

I didn't know what to say or even think. I took a look. It didn't look too far down. The drop fed us into another gully that looked as if it ran straight to a tram pillar, some way off in the distance. If we could just get to there we would be safe. Home and dry. I really didn't want to go back to where we had come from, and climbing up was definitely out of the question. I had that horrible premonition of disaster back. Neither of us knew what to do. The night was definitely coming in. Staying put and waiting for a rescue, having completely strayed from our route didn't seem to be a good option either. Nobody knew where we were on this mountainside. I tried to think clearly and assess each option for the pros and cons, but this was easier said than done. Although I was in a better frame of mind compared to when I was on top of the boulder, I was exhausted. My brain was running through each option quickly; I saw each one as a picture on a postcard and it was flicking from one to another, but I was unable to come to a decision.

Mike took a closer look at what was below us. It seemed to be made up of a series of descending ledges. None of them were very big and it was never far from one to another. Most importantly it looked as if they went all the way to the bottom. He made a plan for us to hop from one to another. He would descend below me and guide me down. If we committed ourselves it would be the quickest and easiest way off the mountain. We decided to give it a try.

At first it went well. The ledges were about eighteen inches wide so you could walk along them. The steps down were fairly straightforward. Mike seemed to be able to do them with ease. It was like a big staircase. I found them harder and decided to sit on each stair, like a small child climbing down the stairs. Occasionally he would have to help me as I shimmied down one. Then the ledges stopped. I knew I wasn't strong enough to climb back up. Mike took a look. There was a jagged rock face to our right hand side. He suggested that a traverse around it would take us onto better ground, from which we could slide down into the gully below. I could see what he was suggesting, but not how to get there. Mike offered to go first, to show me the way. He took the backpack off and dropped it down the sixty feet or so to the bottom before walking around that last ledge to the face. I didn't dare look down to see what had happened to it.

The face was very steep, but it had lots of grippy looking features and bushes with exposed roots that you could grab. Once Mike started to climb it looked a lot harder. He wasn't finding this as easy as some of the rest of the climbing. I did my best to help, letting him know where he could move hands and feet, when I could see them. Then he rounded a corner and disappeared from sight. There was a pause before he began to encourage me to follow. I took a deep breath. Seeing Mike struggle had not given me confidence that I could get around. At a couple of points he had gasped in a way that suggested he was likely to fall. I've never been one to back down from a challenge and there seemed to be no other option so I took a deep breath and turned the cap I was wearing backwards so the peak was facing away from the mountain. It was a symbol I used to show that I meant business when I was in my boat training and I would often do it before an important time trial on the river. I walked around to where he had started; I lowered my right foot onto his first foothold and my right hand onto a root. Moving further onto the face I ran out of holds.

"What do I do now?" I called. He told me to try to reach a footing with my right foot. My legs were just not long enough. He suggested I reach out with my right hand to a crack and then go for the foot hold again. I tried but again I couldn't reach anything or feel anything that gave me confidence and my leg just waved about in desperation. My breathing became faster as I tried again but as I stretched out, I felt my body slip slightly. I quickly moved back. Underneath my right foot the rock was crumbling and the root I was holding with my hands began to pull out. Mike's instructions became more and more desperate.

I was stuck for almost five minutes before the inevitable happened. Time stood still, I became calm and trusted to my fortune in my fall. In that moment my life changed.

# 10 LONG ROAD TO RECOVERY

In Albuquerque University Hospital I spent a long, terrible day waiting for my spinal surgery. Every time I spoke to someone the information changed, from going in to surgery in an hour to waiting half the day. I lay in my bed in fear, waiting. I didn't know how to prepare myself for it. It was make or break for my body and I had no idea what lay in store for me. I was entertaining silly thoughts: would I wake up during the surgery? What would it be like afterwards? Every possible scenario was racing through my head. This was my first operation and potentially the first on my road back to recovery. I hated the wait, the longer time ticked on, the more fractious I got. This was the longest nightmare I had ever been in. Doubt crept in: wondering if it would ever end, would the pain never go away? The only positive was that my body was so tired that I was going in and out of sleep. Time was ticking slowly past again. Every second I was awake allowed my mind time to analyse every part of my situation and my imagination was going wild.

The girls gathered round and did their best to keep my spirits up. Sam worked out how long each batch of medication would last and organised the medical staff. I overheard her laying down the law and making sure I always had what I needed. Eventually someone arrived to explain my surgery and get me to sign the consent form. I was too drugged up to understand him properly. I heard him tell me that there was a possibility I wouldn't walk again. Everything shut down again. He was trying to explain that they would need to graft bone from my hip into my neck to fix my cracked vertebra but I just couldn't understand it. Kim was with me and did her best to translate from medical to the almost childish range my brain was operating on. Eventually they felt that they had got enough information through to me and asked me to sign a consent form.

I had a hierarchy of fears. From not waking up afterwards, through being able to walk again, to not having my head and neck in a mental frame if it went well. At the end of all the discussion there was little choice: a pen was put in my hand and to my shock, I couldn't grip the pen. Kim quickly came to the rescue before my brain went into overdrive, and between the two of us, I made a mark that must have looked enough like my signature and they took me off immediately.

I was taken into a room which was full of very bright white lights. I no longer had the safety of the girls around me and I felt quite lonely, lying on the bed. The surgeon came out to look at me and went into an angry rant at the medics around him. "Why wasn't she brought in when she got here? Why have you waited?" It brought home to me that this really was very serious and that whatever else I had understood I needed the surgery. I must have said something because he followed it up by talking directly to me.

"Don't worry, I'll look after you." He said it in such a calm and touching way that I immediately felt I could trust him, and that he really would look after me. That was the last thing I remembered before I slid down into the embrace of the anaesthetic. The operation would last somewhere between four and six hours. An operation to realign a spine is a very delicate process. During my operation they took a bone graft from my hip to fix the damaged C4 vertebra and wired the two spinous processes of C5 and C6 that had been dislocated or, using the medical terminology, jump shot. They had to be careful not to damage the spinal cord further.

I woke to someone tapping my hand and demanding my attention. It was good to know that I was alive but I wasn't up to cooperating any more than that. They wanted me to open my eyes and drink, but I was happy lying still. The nurse moistened my lips and persuaded me to take a mouthful of a liquid. It was cool and wet but it tasted brown and disgusting. I spat it back out in the same way a small child would. I tried to open my eyes but the room was far too bright. I closed them again, but not before noticing that I didn't have a frame around my head. This was good news. I was addressing my challenges in sequence: the first had been to wake up and the second was not to have a frame. Two down; I was ecstatic, although I'm not sure I let the nurses know.

They had so many demands: wake up; drink; open my eyes; now they wanted me to talk. They tricked me by telling me that my friends wanted to see me. I replied that I didn't want to see them. I've tried hard to understand what happened inside my head over those few days. I had taken a bad fall, nearly died in the night on the mountain, I had been reheated and repaired in the hospital. It was almost as if I was starting a new life. I was reborn on the operating table. From here on I had a life. In the recovery room I was accelerated to toddler stage and I was ready to have a major tantrum if they didn't leave me alone. I was going to do what I wanted to do and that was that.

When I surfaced again I could hear another patient and a medic working in the room. The patient was groaning, which bothered me a little, but there wasn't anything I could do about that and I didn't want to join in. The medics were listening to cowboy music. Country and Western has never been one of my favourites but nearly everyone in the area seemed to listen to it. He stopped what he was doing and came over to try to wake me up.

"Come on, you need to start waking up a bit more. It's time to start talking." I decided that if I had to I would make my presence felt.

"I don't like your music."

"Oh, right. Well what music would you like?" He gave a little chuckle as he said this.

"I don't know. I want to sing."

"What would you like to sing?"

"I don't want to sing your music." My bed was covered in Teddy Bears. I still don't know how I had so many. I think some had come from the hospital and others from the girls. There was one in my hand, I'm not sure how I had got to hold it and it triggered a memory. Today I'm not sure I remember the words, but at that point I knew every word and I sang Teddy Bears Picnic at the top of my voice. I could hear the people around me laughing. It was a lovely sound, but it wasn't enough. I made them sing with me too. After a while they sang their own songs but the recovery ward became a very happy place. The medic stopped singing for a moment and asked whether my friends, who were just outside, could come in to see me now.

"Only if they sing to." I heard him relay the instruction and Kim agree while everyone giggled. The next thing I knew Kim was singing with me. I couldn't see their faces. My eyes were still closed, but it was enough for the hospital. They moved me from recovery back to my care ward. We must have turned a lot of heads, singing our way through the corridors of the Hospital. I don't remember seeing anybody's face, but I heard a lot of laughter before I went back to sleep.

That evening I woke up again. The world was a much less welcoming place this time. Kim and Mike were sitting with me but I wasn't singing. The pain relief must have worn off because I was in agony. They called the hospital staff who went to work, changing bags and drips. They then turned me to check the dressings on my neck and it all hurt too much. I began to scream. This upset Mike and Kim who tried to intervene. The pain was much more intense than it had been on the mountain; there the cold had been overwhelming but the pain was localised. Now it should have gone but instead it seemed to be spread all over my body. Mike physically tried to stop them from moving me and both he and Kim were removed from the room. Kim promised to behave herself and they let her back in to hold my hand.

For the first time I was aware of them giving me morphine. From the injection site in my left arm I felt a warming, reassuring fire spread down to my fingers and up, into my body, relieving me and taking the pain away. It didn't help my head: I was immobile and helpless and I knew I couldn't take it anymore. My hysterical state affected Kim. I could hear her voice breaking as she stroked my hand. It took her some time to calm me down. Eventually I drifted back into sleep.

When I woke again I had Sam with me. I could hear her reading something aloud and was reassured by her presence. She clearly knew what had happened earlier and was ready to manage me. She took charge from that time on, working out how long each pain relief shot would last, monitoring my bags and badgering the medical staff to keep them on top of my needs. I only have vague memories of this time as I wandered in and out of sleep. I didn't know when day turned into night or when the night turned into a new day.

The girls let me know that my parents would be arriving in a number of hours. They tried to make me presentable; washing what skin was still exposed. I still looked like I had jumped and rolled in a mud bath. My feet were cold and they found me some brightly coloured socks. There were occasional updates as they changed flights or were delayed and sent messages to the girls.

Mike and Annamarie went to meet them, bringing them straight back to the hospital. My Dad came in first. Despite the girls best efforts I heard him gasp with shock. Mum followed him in.

It was a moment I was both longing to have and one I had been dreading. Was she disappointed with me? I was with myself. Would she tell me off? I wanted to tell myself off.

"Come on now, what have you been up to." She said it in a jovial way. I can still see her face, the first one I remember seeing since my operation. I had tried so hard to be strong and in control of myself. I had given over control of my body to the medics, who had automated everything with bags and catheters. I was a hyperactive outdoors woman, now immobilised on a bed with a view of a white square panelled ceiling. Control of my response was all I had left. Now the emotions I had held back came out in a rush. My friends tactfully left us alone and Mum nursed me until I slept again. My Mum brought the comfort, the love and tenderness that only a Mother can bring to her child. As the tears came, my Mum just held me.

It was months later that my Mum shared her diaries with me about that first encounter. They described how I looked far more ropey and worse than either of them had imagined. Both my parents were aware of the possible consequences of the operation. They had discussed the worst case options, if I was a 'vegetable' and what as an active person would be the best option. It is hard for me to comprehend how hard that conversation would have been when they agreed that, if necessary, they would switch off the life support machine. My memory of her face does not show one ounce of her inner turmoil.

I woke up some time in the middle of the night. My friends were wonderful. As I drifted up into consciousness I could hear a voice talking to me. Jen was there, wide awake and reading to me. During the day they had started reading a Harry Potter book to me and there she was still reading it. Reassured that I was not alone I let myself drop back down into sleep. It was only afterwards that I discovered the price my friends paid for this care. There was always one of them there, dashing in from attending or between classes at the University; staying up all night in shifts to make sure that I was never alone

The next morning the world began to come into more perspective. I knew I had survived two major life threatening experiences. I had fallen off a mountain and I had been through hours of major surgery. There was no threat to my life anymore but I had been so focussed on survival that I didn't know how to start on recovery. Everything had been taken away from me. The smallest of movements was agony. My neck was immobilised and I was already bored with staring at a ceiling. I was dependant on other people for everything. I had even been catheterised which meant that I had no control of even my most basic functions. Worse still I didn't understand what any of it meant. They had taken a drain out of my neck. I had no idea why a human would have a drain, did that mean things were worse than I had thought or better? I felt helpless and powerless and began to sink into an uncharacteristic self-pity.

For the next two days I lay still and was fed and distracted by my family and friends. They did their best to cheer me up but every difficulty just seemed to make things harder. Even feeding me was tough but also brought some much needed light relief. Coordinating their hands with my mouth seemed to be an impossible task, usually leaving my face coated in jello. Feeding took many hours due to my inability to open my mouth very wide. I would get tired and fall asleep from eating. A cube of jello literally provided much entertainment.

I spoke to my sister and also my uncle in New Zealand

who both started with a jokey "What have you done now?" It didn't help me. I felt that I had been incredibly stupid for getting into that situation and falling on the mountain. I didn't understand that they were trying to make light of my injuries to help us all cope with them. Dr Mike Sheeser, my surgeon came to see me and gave me a prognosis: the operation had gone well and I could expect to recover, but I would be in a hospital bed for three months and in rehabilitation for another three months. My spirits sank even lower. I wouldn't be going home any time soon. I had jeopardised everything that mattered to me – my university degree, my paddling career, everything. I was annoyed with myself and with Mike and there didn't seem to be anything I could do about it.

Things changed the next morning. A physical therapist came to see me with the intention of getting me moving. She used my sheets to move me around and move me on to my left side. It was an incredibly painful process. Everything hurt. My hands were too heavy to lift. Just getting me into a sitting position was too hard and I told her so. I couldn't make her understand that I needed to rest. It was what the surgeon had told me to do and I just wanted to be left alone to do it. Everything was impossible. I didn't want to cooperate, it hurt me too much. Eventually we reached a point where she couldn't continue. I was returned to my static position in my now rumpled bed. As she left she delivered a line that made a huge impression.

"You know what? You have to want to get better."

I was really taken aback by those words. It seemed very harsh. Did she not know what I had been through? How much I was hurting? I began the afternoon brooding on those words and they began to get through to me. They were true; I had to want to get better. I needed to buck my ideas up. I wanted to be with my friends from university. In my conversation with my sister she had tried to prepare me for not going back, for missing a year while

I recovered. My stubbornness began to kick in. If I missed a year my friends would graduate without me. I had been going to my sport lectures with Catrin from the very first day. How would she cope without me? More to the point, how would I cope without her? I had a goal now. I was determined that I would get back to university with the minimum delay. Focussing my mind had a powerful effect on me. It wasn't all easy after that, but whenever things were hard or painful I refocused myself on that goal and things would get better.

The days that followed are a bit of a blur. There were, however, some significant milestones. A different physical therapist came back the next day. I'm not sure whether it was recovery, determination or her using a different method to help me up but it didn't hurt nearly as much. It was an achievement. My mood improved every day. My friends were always there, bringing laughter and light relief. The feeding cubes of jello continued and the more I was able to take in of what was going on around me the funnier I found it. Watching them try to feed me, failing to suppress the urge to make the open mouth gestures that we make for babies made us all giggle. Mum, Dad, Sam, Jen and Kim would read to me. My Mum was especially good at changing her tone of voice for different characters. I personally just liked hearing her voice; the words and story were irrelevant. It brought back and re-established happy memories from when I was a young child when she would read to me in bed or on the sofa. We had one of the Harry Potter books and hard as I tried I couldn't concentrate properly on it. Each time they opened the book they would prompt me to establish where the previous reader had finished, but I could never remember. They read me the first chapter of that book so often that they must have memorised large parts of it.

With each day that passed I did a little more. The therapist helped me onto crutches. I took a single step and collapsed back into a chair. It was the first step I'd taken since I'd climbed onto the rock face on Sandia Mountain and it was the cause of a major celebration. To celebrate my friends bought me a chicken sub and spent the evening rolling it into pea sized balls and feeding it to me. We laughed between ourselves that the chicken would enhance my recovery as it couldn't have its usual effect of making me super hyperactive to the extent I would normally bounce literally from place to place. They also decorated my ceiling in a Hawaiian luau style to give me something more interesting to look at. News was spreading slowly. I didn't want many people to know because I still felt stupid, but friends had to know. Their messages of support kept me going. I still have some of them. Catrin emailed me with an offer to help me get around when I got home. She instructed the girls to feed me jaffa cakes, which was one of my favourite treats at the time.

Things were gradually getting better. I began to be able to walk with the aid of crutches. I could only put weight on one leg but it gave me mobility, and with mobility came extra freedoms. Once I had some mobility my catheter was removed giving me more control of my life. Each small step forward was celebrated, but it also brought frustrations. I was still unable to do so many basic things. I began to worry about how I might cope. Small things like how I might put on trousers or do up my shoes when I couldn't reach my toes; how would I brush my hair when I couldn't reach my hands behind my back became major concerns. My friends tried to help me, to give me solutions, but each one only made way for another problem.

I took my frustrations out on Mike. He was often with me, in the room, saying very little. He seemed to be very low. Perhaps it was a symptom of survivor's guilt, but I didn't recognise it at the time. So many things were going through my mind. How had we gone so wrong? Why hadn't we simply retraced our steps? I couldn't explain any of this to myself, let alone anyone else. A week after the accident I brought matters to a head and asked him. I was alone with Mike. He was sitting quietly picking thorns out of his hands and couldn't look me in the eye. We couldn't communicate any more. He was locked up in himself, his body language was closed. I told him to leave me. It was a very painful time, the end of a very close friendship. I think we were focussed on our own traumatic memories of that day and if we couldn't communicate anymore there was no way out of it.

Moving was a good thing. Every time I got out of bed and walked it helped my recovery. On day three the doctors reduced my expected hospital time by a month. Five months until I might get home. Initial expectations for intensive care had been for two weeks, but they moved me out after five days. They removed my catheter so that I was able to move and had control of my own bladder. Boom, my expected time in hospital came down by another month. It all made me very happy. Two days later I was only expected to be in hospital for another week. It was down to three months to go. I was ecstatic. I began to feed myself. This was my last step out of toddler stage. Every gain in movement was a step towards my goal of getting back to my real life. I began to get visits from the reps for the rehab centres. I wasn't very pleased by this. I had been given a zimmer frame, something I associated with being elderly and immobile. I hated it. Now the reps were coming and talking about multi-terrain mobility units and exercise regimes. It was all too slow and I didn't want to go. Each time they came my mood took a turn for the worse. I would give in to negative thinking while they were there, but as soon as they left my stubbornness kicked in. I wouldn't be going into rehab. I could walk ten metres now and rehab times were coming down by the day. I was determined to make it. I just wanted to go home.

I became obsessed about not being able to do what I thought were the most trivial things. I was desperate to go home, yet my body was still not working or improving at a pace that was fast enough for me. One particular task I couldn't do was go to the toilet on my own. Trying to sit with a broken pelvis was very painful. I couldn't put my weight on my right side or right leg. I found it so undignified and what should be a simple task was very painful. It only added fuel to my frustrations and the depression I was sinking into. I had to hold on to my goal with every small strand of hair that I could find.

On the Friday the hospital staff were ready to discharge me. They had come around to the idea that I might not need rehab. I lit up with joy. If I could fly I could get back to University, even if I was late. I wanted so desperately to get back to a proper life. Any help that seemed to delay that goal wasn't worthwhile. I needed a release. The physical therapist arranged for me to be taken to the hospital gym where other people in recovery were working. I was taken down in a wheelchair being the stubborn person I am I attempted to wheel myself, but only veered off to one side of the corridor as my left side was stronger and more coordinated than my right. When I got into the gym, it lifted my state of mind. It didn't feel like I was in a hospital and people were mostly wearing real clothes rather than just hospital gowns. Although I couldn't do anything with any of the equipment the atmosphere sparked another goal. I would get back to fitness.

Mum had been spending a lot of time on the phone to the insurance companies and medical staff in the UK. In order for me to go home I had to have suitable transport and a specialist in England into whose care they could discharge me. A medical secretary friend of my Mum's made a lot of phone calls for me. Eventually they located Professor Dowell who agreed to take my case. Things were changing almost by the hour. There was talk of a special medical plane to fly me home. I didn't like the sound of that. Like rehab it sounded as if I would be treated as a victim. The hospital weighed in on my side – being strapped down in a bed on the plane for that long wouldn't be good for me. I needed to be able to walk. Eventually the insurers and hospital agreed a plan to fly over a specially trained medical cabin crew member to accompany me home in first class cabins where I would have a lot of space. The only question now was when. On Friday I was expected to go into rehab for a month before I would fly home. On the Saturday morning I managed to walk the length of the corridor and back again, as well as managing a small step. For the first time I wore hospital trousers with the gown, it felt like proper clothes and was another step towards getting back my life. When I was examined later that day they decided that I was making such good progress they could discharge me to fly home as soon as possible.

I had achieved my goal. Every worry and challenge along the way had bothered me, but from the moment my therapist had told me that I had to want to get better, I had never considered that I wouldn't get back to University. In a phone call with my sister she had tried to prepare me for having to go back to University a year late. I responded with characteristic determination. From that moment it became an overriding goal: university and rehab were incompatible.

On the Saturday I had a final meeting with Dr Mike Sheeser, my surgeon. I really couldn't thank him enough for what he had done for me. I made a point of having my picture taken with him: this was one picture I didn't mind having taken. My mum had taken pictures throughout my stay in hospital to remind me where I had come from, I had argued with her and pleaded with her not to take them. I am now glad I have some pictorial evidence.

"I've never known anyone like you. Your recovery has been remarkable," he told me.

"I think it's the chicken," I replied. It puzzled him, but it made my friends and family laugh. I had beaten all the expectations. From an original prognosis of six months in hospital and rehab I was going to be going home in less than two weeks. He gave me a big hug before he let me go.

"You have an aim," he said, "that has made a lot of difference. Go for it."

I was discharged to my friend Annamarie's home. It was close to both the Hospital and the Airport. I could be there for up to a week while they arranged flights. My family had been staying there but my Dad had flown back to the UK before I was discharged to aid preparations for my return. It had suitable accommodation for me as it was a bungalow which meant I could get around more easily. I expected to be there for a number of days, but things were still moving rapidly. After our first night Mum received a call from the insurers to tell us that we could fly the next day. We quickly arranged a farewell dinner for my wonderful friends. Sam was unable to join us, but we had a fabulous meal together. Sam surprised me in the morning by coming over to see me before the flight. We shed a few tears. Throughout my time in hospital she had been my rock. Whenever I really needed someone she had been there, holding my hand or harrying the hospital staff for information and help. I was going to have to cope without her now and that was a daunting prospect.

The journey back consisted of two flights. Mike was with us on the first one, but flying tourist class. We said goodbye to him at the next airport and made our way to the first class lounge. Neither of us had ever flown first class before. For me it was simply something I had to get through, but for Mum it was a wonderful adventure. There were very few of us in the first class compartment. We were put onto the plane first to make sure that I was settled in properly and then the rest of the plane was loaded. It was a night flight and I was expecting to sleep for most of it. We had seats that converted into beds, but I wasn't allowed to lie down until the plane had taken off.

From that moment much of the cabin activity was focussed around us. Mum was excited that our food would be cooked fresh and not brought out in airline trays. I slept most of the time. Every so often they would wake me up and I walked around the cabin. The walks were major undertakings for all of us. First we had to contact the Captain to ensure that there would be no likelihood of turbulence while I was on my feet. Then the cabin doors were closed and I was led on a circuit, with Mum in front of me and my Medical Attendant behind. We must have looked very strange, but I never did find out what the other passengers thought of our strange parade.

I loved my visits to America, but both years it seemed I was destined to return in dramatic circumstances. The first time I was desperate to get home in the chaos that surrounded the destruction of the World Trade Centre. This time the drama was of my own making. Once again I was simply pleased to be home and one step closer to my goal of getting back to my life and University.

# 11 HOMECOMING

Landing at the end of a flight is a strange experience. Mingled with the excitement of arriving at your destination is the knowledge that you aren't really there. There is always another stage to the journey. The hurdles of bureaucracy still have to be overcome before you transfer to your home or destination. Arriving as a medical patient should be a smoother ride but being a stubborn patient who desperately wanted her independence was only going to make it even worse.

They let the other passengers off the plane before letting the ambulance crew on to collect me. This brought us our next problem. They couldn't get their stretcher through the doors of the plane. I wanted to walk off the plane, on my own two feet. It would have made me feel independent and in control of my life. It was much less fuss and would draw less attention to me. It wasn't to be. The medics were adamant. The insurance conditions meant that I had to leave the plane on a stretcher. I did not want that and argued with them, but to no avail. Eventually a solution was reached and I was taken off the plane on a baggage lift, sitting up, with my arms crossed and scowl on my face.

The ambulance crew were delightful. They had a Satnav, the first that Mum and I had ever seen or heard and we played with it all the way home. The highlight of the journey was reaching the Dartford Crossing and lighting up the blue lights to pass through the tunnel for free. Despite the sleeps I had on the plane and in the ambulance, when I got home I was exhausted, although I didn't want to admit it. I made my point, though, and walked up the drive to the house. The ambulance men were lovely. They stayed for a drink and to make sure I was comfortable. As they left I heaved a huge sigh. From that moment the insurance machine that had driven my life for nearly two weeks and had interfered with any decision I made stopped. Without the insurance I could never have accessed the level of care I had in America and I will always appreciate that I had it, but my stubborn nature wanted to get on with recovery and do it my way. Now I could. I gave in to my stubbornness and headed into my new downstairs bedroom. I dropped into an exhausted sleep.

When I awoke I was in a world that was both strange and familiar. Tim had cleared out the dining room and turned it into a bedroom for me. I was back in the real world and it was colder and quieter than Albuquerque. I missed Sam, Jen and Kim but their absence was compensated by my brother and the family dog that couldn't wait to see me. My Mum came into me a few times to try to rouse me. I just wanted to continue sleeping. Finally after a lot of persuasion I got up and we had a family meal together to celebrate. It was wonderful to be sitting at a table. It's a prominent landmark in my recovery. I sat in a sterilised plastic garden chair, the only kind I found to be comfortable.

Before I knew it, the sun had gone to bed and it was time for me to do the same. I was unsettled for the first night. Sam had made sure that I had never been alone since the accident and for the first time I was alone again.

Hospitals are never really dark or silent, but the dining room was both. I woke in the night with the beginnings of a panic attack. I was stuck flat on my back, with nothing I could grab on to, to help roll myself over onto my side. I was frightened. Fortunately Mum had thought ahead and set up a baby monitor to let her know what was happening so she was with me quickly. Then she had a brainwave and moved the dog's bed into my room. Whenever I woke after that her presence would reassure me. I would talk to Sally, the dog, telling her all my secrets.

The house fell quickly back into its normal routine. My brother would come down to see me in the mornings before school despite Mum's warnings that he should leave me to sleep. I felt like a zombie. I was instantly battling tiredness and my inability to do the little things that would make me feel normal. Mum talked to me all the time, in the way that you talk to a small child, mostly in the mornings. Sometimes it annoyed me. Mostly it made me giggle, especially when she washed behind my ears with a face cloth.

On my first full day home I had to go to my doctors for a first visit. My wounds were checked and sadly my leg wound was infected. The nurse cleaned the wound and then dressed it to keep it clean. This bothered me. The Americans had instructed that it should be left open to speed the healing. I couldn't deal with the change. It made me angry but to no avail, the doctor added antibiotics to my drug regime which felt like a step backwards.

My Grandparents came to visit the next day. We had difficulty trying to get them to understand just what had happened on the mountainside. They went through a range of responses, some appropriate and some less so. What was clear was just how much I meant to them and how difficult it would have been for the family if I had been killed. Eventually we understood each other but the whole visit was exhausting. It also reinforced my impression that my own stupidity had caused my fall. I was still confined to the downstairs of the house but by now I was able to move about much more, using my crutches to move around the house, trying to become more mobile. I was hard work but Mum never once complained.

On Friday we went into Chelmsford and met with my new Consultant. Professor Dowell looked, to me, like a mad scientist. He was tall and thin, with wiry flyaway hair. I didn't take to him immediately. His manner was academic and professional. I had grown fond of Dr Sheeser in Albuquerque. He had saved my spine and now I had to trust a new surgeon, who seemed very different. He sat me down and immediately took my neck brace off, followed by the wound dressing with some of my hair still attached. This sent me into a panic. I had been told not to remove it unless I was lying down and I was afraid that my neck would collapse or something similar without it. It was completely irrational, but nothing was making sense in my brain and I was in sensory overload.

He took a good long look. My X-rays hadn't followed me across the Atlantic so he sent me for some more before we met up again in his consulting room. He took a long look at them and then pushed his glasses up his nose. After a pause he told me that Dr Sheeser had done an excellent job on my neck, although we would have gone about it in a different way in the UK. We made an appointment to go back in a week and then he took away my crutches. I was very dismayed. I had just begun to cover a decent distance every day and I was worried about my mobility. Americans use crutches that support you under your armpit, but the British prefer a crutch that fits to your forearms because it transfers weight differently. He gave me a pair in the British design. Now I was going to have to learn to use them all over again. I was a little discouraged when we left for home.

Claire, my sister, came to visit the next day. She took

over with me completely. We had never been that close, adapting to our disjointed childhood by becoming insular and independent women. She blew into the house and took the pressure off Mum by entertaining me. It was clear that she had been worrying about me but she spoke to me as if nothing had happened. It was what I needed. I began to feel normal and from that day my relationship with Claire began to change. It was the first step on a long journey but we both began to open up and have become a lot closer.

Claire organised for me to take a shower. The shower was upstairs and it was a place I had not yet dared to go to, as a whole flight of stairs was quite a daunting prospect to negotiate on my crutches. It was worth it, it was a moment of pure pleasure and escape. The warm water ran down my back and took my stress away along with the dirt and sweat. The feel of the water took me off, as it does when I'm on a river, to a happy place amongst the chaos of life. I gave a little smile as the soothing sprinkling of water ran over my body. It removed me from where I was, the fact I was sitting on an upturned waste bin and the embarrassment I felt that my mum was washing my hair as well as my body. Once clean, my mum could see how content I was and just let me have a private few minutes. Mum had been keeping me clean with wet wipes which allowed me to feel fresh, but it just wasn't the same as the power and feeling of cleanliness that came from a shower head. Even though I had had a shower when in America, my hair was still not properly clean and it was good to get the rest of the detritus of Sandia Mountain out of it. It was bliss, but every little thing I wanted to do was long drawn out and complicated. The effort required for me to get to the shower and sit in it led to me needing a nap, once I was dry. Perhaps the freshness and warmth of being wrapped in towels afterwards made me feel sleepy to. After my nap, my neck brace needed to be removed again so dry padding could replace the wet ones. The whole process made me nervous as well as my Mum who had to perform the task. As she did it, I could see her eyes scan me up and down then when the task was complete, she smiled to reassure me it was all going to work out ok eventually. Here, in Mum's house I was more determined than ever that I would be back at University when the term started.

After Claire's visit I increased my efforts to become more mobile. I set myself targets walking down the street in front of the house. The first was to reach the first lamppost, approximately 25m from the front door. When I reached it I had to take a rest before I turned back. The next day I screwed up my resolve and walked two lampposts before turning around. I began to email my friends. I needed to start facing the world around me, especially if I wanted to get back to being a part of it. I had kept a tight control of what I told the world. I was afraid that my injuries told the world that I had been stupid for falling down a mountain.

Paul Anderson, my Canoe Coach and friend, was the first to visit me. I was keen to see him, he was already an influential figure in my life, but I was also somewhat embarrassed by my injuries. In the end the embarrassment won out when he arrived and I hid in the back room until he came in to get me. Paul has a very sharp intelligence. He was clearly shocked to see me on crutches and in a neck brace but he quickly recovered himself. He knew instinctively that I didn't want to go through another blow by blow account of my fall and we talked for ages about Newton's Laws of Motion. He put time into helping me work out my terminal velocity as I hit the ground and began bouncing, distracting me with the kind of maths that I love. Paul is a strong exponent of the need to plan. He is always full of plans for what he will do next. He asked the important question of me. Did I have one? I didn't really; just an overpowering need to get back to my life. I had the goal, I just didn't know how to get there. He inspired me; the next day I began extending my daily walks further.

Pete was my other visitor that week.

I had last seen him when Mike and I climbed out of his van in Dallas, Texas. I wasn't sure how it would go. Working side by side all summer at Camp was a very intense experience and we had become very close. The short time apart had turned that closeness into what has proved to be a deep and lasting friendship. We spent a lovely afternoon reminiscing and looking at his photographs. Walking together we got as far as a parade of local shops, about 400m. I rested on a bench while Pete bought us a snack before we walked back home. It was a strong motivator. I was more convinced than ever that I would be able to get back to University.

Whilst things were going well with physical recovery there was less progress with my mental one. I was very frustrated. There was so much that I still wanted to do, that I had taken for granted before the accident. At times, when I couldn't raise my hands enough to do simple things like tie a pony tail, wipe my bottom or tie my shoes getting back to university seemed absolutely impossible. I was still in touch with Mike. On the Thursday we spoke on a mobile phone that he had bought me. He wasn't very responsive and my frustration boiled over. I couldn't understand why he wasn't embracing life with both hands. He hadn't fallen from the mountain, I had. He could do so much but he appeared to be moping around. My temper boiled over again and we argued. He told me that looking at me reminded him of what had happened on the mountain and he could never look at me again. I ended the call and threw the phone onto the floor.

With the benefit of hindsight I can see his problems now. He had suffered the trauma of watching me fall away from him on the mountain, endured a bruising run down to get help and then sat helplessly waiting, hoping I wouldn't die, as they searched the hillside all night. He had been the first to see the extent of my injuries in hospital. It must have been very traumatic. At the time, though, none of that meant anything to me. I didn't want to blame him but I did want to understand why he had driven me so hard on the mountain, I would never have driven anyone that hard in a kayak, and I wasn't getting any answers. I can see that I am a living reminder of that day but I don't have that reaction to him. I still struggle with the rejection. On that day it sent me over the top. I went into the anger phase of my recovery and he became its target. I marched into the living room on my crutches and threw a toddler like tantrum at my mother. I hurled my crutches at the floor and shouted and cried, listing all the things I couldn't do and wanted to. It wasn't just the little things. I couldn't paddle or exercise to vent my frustration and it all spilled over. Eventually I came to a shuddering halt as I added not being able to pick up my crutches and therefore move to the list of things I couldn't do, but before I could for myself.

She sat in the armchair and listened to my moans. Then after a long pause, smiled and asked if I had finished. I replied with a child toned, "Yes" Followed by a bit of silence and, "Could I have a hug?"

Together we began to make a plan. I had a mobile phone that Mike had given me and I sent Tim into the garden with it with a hammer. I may not have been able to hit it myself but seeing Tim destroy it for me was a big help. The next day was Friday and I was due back in to see Professor Dowell. As long as things went well we would shake things up a bit at the weekend.

This time I was more prepared for the visit to my Nutty Professor and he was both warmer with me and more encouraging. He had the x-rays and scans from America. He made a remark about the amount of radiation I had been exposed to for all those x-rays, CT scans and MRIs. It made me chuckle and I began to warm to him. He looked carefully at my pelvis and neck and was very pleased with my progress. It was now just over 3 weeks since it happened. I told him that I wanted to return to University in just over a week. I really expected him to tell me that it was impossible. My family had been trying to manage my expectations ever since I had come out of hospital. Instead he told me that he would see how I was progressing, and that we would make a decision next week, but that with my positive and determined attitude it was possible, as long as I was able to fend for myself. I seized this hope with both hands and began to revise my negative impression of him. We arranged another appointment for the next week.

At the weekend my family put the distract Gilly plan into action. I was loaded carefully into Tim's car and we set off for the coast. Before I found Canoeing I had done Sailing for a couple of years and they had a daring plan. We were going to sail. Tim had a good friend with a small yacht and I was to be the guest starter of a race. This meant actually going into the boat and leaving the bank. It was the nearest I was going to get to an adventure and, even better, it was on water. Tim brought me by a roundabout route, on country roads, to the Marina, building the feeling of adventure. As he pulled into the car park the sound of sheets and blocks tapping on masts raised my excitement level and I walked carefully over the pontoons to the boat. Just getting me onto it was an exercise in careful ingenuity. I was eventually lifted and eased over the rail and deposited upright in a corner of the yacht's cockpit. We were ready and set off. To keep me safe we only used the motor but it was enough. We held position against a marker buoy and I was given the horn to start the race. It was everything I needed. I wasn't keen to be seen, my crutches and neckbrace marked me out as someone who had taken a foolish fall, but at the same time I was actually out, in the open air, and taking part in the adventurous and active life that I craved. My morale was lifted and I was more determined than ever that I would make it back to University.

With this attitude and the now real hope that I might get to University my walks improved rapidly. I joined Mum on a trip to collect my brother from school. It was quite a long walk for me and I set off early to make sure I could get there and to give me time for a rest on arrival. I made good time and was let in to the school. I found it a difficult experience. This was the primary school that I had left, only a handful of years ago. Many of the teachers knew me and my family. By now they knew what had happened and I became the centre of interest. They were shocked to see me, both for the extent of my injuries and the way in which I seemed to be recovering. One of them even wanted to hug me which I found very difficult. Whilst they were doing it to show their genuine care for me, I was embarrassed. I still felt that my fall was the result of my own stupidity. When Josh, Mum and I were finally able to go we walked home very slowly.

Going back to university was my goal, but making the calls I needed to arrange it was daunting. I was convinced that falling off a mountain would give me a reputation for stupidity. I plucked up my courage and rang the university administration. Their first response was to tell me that it would be fine to take a break for a year. It took me a little while to convince them that no, I didn't want a year off. I just might be a little late. They were prepared to support any decision I made. This was exciting. I wasn't chasing a false hope. If I could persuade Professor Dowell, I could go back to university.

Later that day Mum called me to the phone. My friend Sharon was calling. After our meeting at the camp in America she had gone travelling and had just returned home to a flood of emails about my accident. It didn't help her that I took some time to come to the phone and that only served to increase her anxiety. When I finally got there she was distraught. Sharon had been the last of my university friends to see me before my fall. I had been at the height of fitness, bursting with irrepressible energy. It was a very emotional call. She promised that she would gather a group of my friends and they would visit me the first weekend they were back. I'm certain she didn't believe it was possible for me to be back by then. I found the call difficult. I knew how much I valued my friends, but I hadn't realised how much they might care about me.

A couple of days later I was still progressing well. I was doing more and more for myself. I picked up the phone to the first of my housemates; Fazia was a very bright girl, with an Afghan mother. We had lived together with Carla the previous year and got on very well. Both of them had very Christian views but had never had a problem with my less religious philosophy. We were going to share with another friend, Sue. We exchanged a few pleasantries and then I broached the subject of my problem.

"Fuzz, I'm sorry but I've had a bit of an accident."

"Don't worry. Whatever it is we'll help you."

"It might be quite difficult at first, but I promise, it will get easier." I assumed she had already heard.

"Are you sure, won't it only get harder? It doesn't matter though, we're your friends and we will help you." Fuzz was close to Carla, I knew she could speak for them both. I was puzzled though.

"Thank you. It's not going to get harder, though, I'm improving every day."

"Aren't you pregnant then?" Once we had that misconception straightened out we were amused by it for weeks. I knew that I could rely on my housemates. The relationship I had built with them the previous year allowed me to not put up my usual front of not showing weakness; with them I could just be me.

Now all I needed was Professor Dowell's approval. I went back to him later in the week. Once again he was really impressed by my progress. He sat me on his bed and began a series of mobility tests on my body, checking out my range of movement and the effect my injuries were having on my coordination and the power in my limbs. Somehow I was able to carry out movements and combinations of movements for him that I hadn't been able to do before, and some of which I wouldn't be able to do for weeks yet. The most memorable one was lifting my whole leg off the bed in one go whilst on my back; it took me months to be able to do it again. We made my next appointment for just less than two weeks time and he gave me his blessing to go to University.

We left the next day, four weeks after my fall. I could hardly believe it. I had gone from expecting to spend three months in hospital and three in rehab to getting my life back in one month. It wasn't going to be easy, but I knew that if I could beat that diagnosis I could achieve anything.

# 12 BACK TO LIFE

My first evening back at University was a lovely experience. My housemates, Sue, Fazia and Carla were excited to see me. Mum took them aside to give them instructions on how to make sure I was kept safe before unpacking everything for me. I was left alone in a new room. Somehow it was both familiar and strange at the same time. It was missing my most important possessions – all my paddling and outdoor sports gear. There had been an assumption that I wouldn't be needing any of it for a while. I spent that first evening with my old friends and getting to know Sue. There was no doubt about their support. They offered to help in any way they could and Sue, who I hardly knew at that time, offered me limitless lifts in her car.

The next day Sue dropped us onto campus and we walked around the University to run through the registration procedures. There were several offices that we needed to visit. I was on a different course to the others and was dreading having to do things on my own. At a university with a major sports focus it isn't unusual to see people bearing injuries. Crutches, plaster casts and even neck braces are a common sight. They draw attention, though, and I was worried about that. Mine wasn't an injury sustained in a heroic attempt to excel; it was a sign that I had been stupid. I didn't want to have to answer the inevitable questions and began hiding behind my friends wherever possible. I took refuge with their friends – they weren't sports students and they talked about subjects that meant I didn't need to join in or explain.

Going solo to collect my students loan cheque revealed lots of problems that I hadn't anticipated. I struggled to open doors and hold them there while I sorted out my crutches to get through. Carrying a single piece of paper between registration desks without crumpling it was close to reducing me to tears when Carla appeared out of nowhere. She had worked out for herself that I would need help but never ask for it. Lots of small tasks were harder. I found it all very frustrating. I was vulnerable. There were so many students returning from the summer that every space seemed to be crowded with loud, excitable people. Eventually it got too much and I had to leave, almost breaking down in tears as my crutches jammed in a door.

I sent word out to my friends that I was back and as the weekend arrived so did my friends. There was a constant throughput of them, turning up in a variety of states. I received them seated royally in our shared living space, sitting in my desk chair, the only one in which I could be comfortable for an extended period of time. One of them, Ali, a friend from the Canoe Club stayed for the whole evening. Over the next year his support in both study and paddling was going to make a huge difference to me. I began to build a closer bond with Sarah. Her sports career had been brutally terminated by a knee injury and the reconstruction had left her in a similarly immobile state for a while. We discussed some of the difficulties I was having moving parts of my body. She had the same experience and advised me that I would have to think about the movement more before making it. She called it "pre-telling" myself and there are still many movements that require me to do that today.

My reunion with Sharon was the hardest, for both of us. I was very different to the bouncy ball of energy who had visited her in America. I had lost a lot of muscle at a surprising rate in hospital. I knew I looked thin. I was nervous about how upset she had been on the phone the week before. When she finally saw me she rushed across the room to hug me, grabbing me in the only accessible place, and holding my head to her. I had to explain that my neck was still delicate, but the hug was lovely. I had been holding back on contact with my friends in England and this hug was very welcome. All of my friends promised to support me. I was going to need it.

My first lecture was at 9 o'clock on Monday. I allowed myself an hour and a half to walk to it as it was just over a mile away. Sharon was in accommodation on the route. I rang her when I reached her building. Fifteen minutes later she joined me after I had covered about five hundred yards. I was exhausted for the lecture. I remember making notes but I don't remember any of the content. Between lectures was chaos. Every student in the university seemed to be rushing along the corridors I needed to use. My next lecture was on a higher floor. After it I found that I couldn't manage the descent of the stairs. My friends gathered round me and supported me down a ramped route. By Thursday I was completely exhausted. Part way through a morning lecture I closed my eyes and slumped over onto Sally, with Sharon supporting me on the other side. The lecture finished early and I felt an overwhelming relief. I started to reach for my bag and books only to find that my friends were ahead of me, scooping up my possessions and almost having to carry me out. Sarah was dispatched to collect her car. They took me home and propped me up in a chair. My next lecture was in the afternoon and I was determined to go to it.

Sharon was not impressed, but we eventually agreed that she would come back to see how I was and collect me if she felt I was up to it. I slept for the rest of the morning but made it to the lecture. Fortunately it was my last of the week. Surviving my fall had given a real sense of purpose. Getting back to university had been my challenge to get me out of the hospital. Now that I was there I was determined that I would excel. Just sitting at home and seeing my friends was not enough. I wanted first class honours. The only way I knew to achieve it was to put in the hours of work and that started with the lectures. In that first week, I had only missed one lecture. That was because I was physically unable to travel from one end of campus to the other in the ten minutes allocated on the timetable. I tried my best but when, after 30 minutes had passed, I was just half way, I knew my efforts were futile. I'm still not sure how I got through that first week.

For anyone sensible the weekend would have been a chance to recover. I had other ideas. On the Saturday I went for a walk along the canal with Ali. I was trying to build up my stamina. About half way I needed a rest and I sat on the grass at the side. Ali borrowed my crutches to try them. He threw himself comically around the canal bank and inspired me to try waking without them. On the way back I managed without my crutches as much as possible. Ali walked beside me using the crutches, and I held onto his arm to steady myself. We must have looked very comical. In the evening he took me to Nottingham to see Zoey at a Canoeing Training Camp. In the dark of the evening I walked from the car without my crutches, again clutching onto Ali. I tried to disguise how badly I was hurt. I enjoyed the freedom. I spent the Sunday sitting with the Canoe Club at the Fresher's Fair, catching up with old paddling buddies. It was the first time I had seen many of them and word had spread that I had hurt myself, although no-one knew how. While I was there a crack began to show in their confidence in me when it was suggested that my neck brace might put people off trying the sport. The suggestion was soon crushed but it would come back later.

Later that day, Mum collected me and took me back to Essex for a consultation with Professor Dowell. He started with my walking.

"I told you that you could start putting some weight on your leg, as long as it didn't hurt. Have you been doing that?"

"Well, I have been putting some weight on it..."

"You've been walking without your crutches, haven't you?"

I nodded.

"Have you?" Mum sounded shocked. I deliberately hadn't mentioned this to her.

"How far have you been going without them? Show me."

"Well you said I should put weight on it as long as it didn't hurt."

"Yes, how far have been walking?"

"A fair bit."

At that point I knew that he appreciated how much I wanted to get better and we really understood each other. He told me that I could now go without my crutches and sent me down for an x-ray. It was more good news. My neck and pelvis were healing far better than expected and I would be able to go without my neck brace. I was ecstatic. I had been given a prognosis of six months in hospital or recovery and here I was five weeks and five days later, less than six weeks later, removing my brace.

I was shocked and surprised although I think my mum was more shocked than I was. Was I dreaming? I wanted to pinch myself. Instead I did a slow motion blink of my eye lids.

I still had to wear it on car journeys as protection against whiplash, but this was my primary goal, achieved.

Five weeks, five days! We celebrated at Mum's and when Dad came to collect me to take me back he was astounded to see me without my brace, as were my friends when I walked into my house later that evening. From here on I was no longer marked out by my brace and crutches as different to other people. I felt that I had recovered and now I had my life back. Of course it wasn't true. Each step brought me closer to a life I can never have back, but will never stop trying to get. Being released from my brace gave me another burst of optimism. I still had restricted movement in my right leg from my pelvic injury but I knew what to do. I had to exercise. The way to get full movement back was to move. I was now walking, even though it was more of a strange hobble, I was also told I could try swimming, because all my open wounds had healed and I was less susceptible to infection .

Dad dropped me at about ten in the evening. Fuzz and Carla did a double take when I walked in using no crutches and without my brace. I had called my brace and crutches my accessories and now I was free of them.

The first day back started with a maths lecture. I walked in feeling almost normal. I sat between Sharon and Sarah and spent the whole fifty minutes rubbing my neck. I wasn't conscious that I was doing it, but my neck was actually cold. Eventually Sharon pulled my hand away and held it down on the desk to stop me. My neck was rubbed red. Now that my neck was not immobilised, and I was allowed to move my neck I found that I couldn't remember how to. It all felt very strange. The operation on my neck due had left me with reduced movement.

The lectures became my routine. I still needed breaks on short walks but without accessories I no longer stood out. This was both a blessing, as I felt liberated from self consciousness and a curse when people were unaware that I was still suffering. We built a routine around my lectures, using coffee shops and canteens to give me refuge and even letting me sleep in Sharon's room on campus when I needed it.

Caz organised for the two of us to use the college pool on a quiet night. It was a brand new facility with a moveable floor and we used it to make it really shallow for me, so that I could get in. It was my first swim and it took an hour for me to swim six widths. In many ways I wasn't really swimming, I had my left leg in contact with the floor for much of the time; I bounced and drifted across. The feeling of freedom and support that the water gave was much more important in helping me heal than the exercise. After the swim we joined the Canoe Club, for the evening. Nic, one of the new students was also moving around carefully. We formed an instant bond when I found that she was recovering from a dislocated hip. We both had mixed feelings, keen to get back into boats but nervous about whether we would be able to do it.

The next week I got back into a boat. The club's first trip of the academic year was always a loop using the canal and the River Soar, starting from Barrow on Soar. It's a short trip but when it's the first trip for many of the new members it takes a lot longer. The club laid on an open canoe for me, and I sat in the front seat while the guys I had coached in the year before took it in turns to propel me. It was only six and a half weeks after my accident. I wasn't paddling, but I was on the water. I trailed my hand over the side the whole way, reconnecting me with my chosen element. On the way to the river Caz refused to start the van until I put my collar on. I was being naughty, hiding it in my coat, but the whole club looked after me, refusing to let me carry more than a couple of paddles.

The miraculous healing of my body was not mirrored by a healing of my mind. I was so focussed on getting back to mobility and health that I had neglected that completely. I was shut off; I had refused to discuss what had happened with anyone. I was absolutely convinced that Mike and I had been infected by an uncharacteristic madness on the mountain and I was terrified of what people might think of me for it. I hadn't even told my closest friends at the University what had happened, just hidden behind a facile "I lost my footing and fell." I put off seeking any kind of help, in case it meant I would have to explain and open myself up to reproach. I was strong Gilly again, on the outside, but on the inside things were getting much worse. I stopped sleeping at night; nightmares and a feeling of falling taking the place of healing sleep. It still took all my strength just to get to lectures. Once there I was writing notes automatically, battling to stay awake. I needed to get fit again. I also needed to find relief from the nightmares.

Characteristically I took matters into my own hands and decided to call Mike. He had left the university but returned to Loughborough to work so he was still local. Perhaps if we talked it through it would help us both. Mike was the only other person on the mountain with me. Only he could help me track through that day and help me work out why we had persisted in climbing boulders beyond my skill without a rope: pushed on, making poor decision after poor decision until it ended in disaster for me. I couldn't get through to him. I tried several more times before I went for more direct action. I called Ali and he gave me a lift to Mike's house. One of his housemates let me in and I presented myself in his Living Room. All my carefully prepared words deserted me. I felt a desperate mixture of fear, pain and then, slowly, anger. I could see that he was struggling in the same way. I had pushed him away on our return from America and now it seemed there was no way back. Were we both pretending it hadn't happened? Our attempts at communication were poor, but ended when he declared that the only way he could help was to block me out, to pretend that I had died on the mountain.

I must have stood there, speechless for a full five minutes. I was alive! I was in front of him! I had battled hard to live so could he reduce all of that to pretending that I was dead? I had to fight back tears. I had come to see him in an attempt at reconciliation and to try to find out what had happened on the mountainside and he had thrown it back at me. It was a moment almost as dark as those I had experienced on the mountain. I could almost still be there. I had fallen less than two months ago and could still taste the Sandia dust in my mouth.

I walked out of the house and stared up at the sky. It was no more help to me than it had been before. I looked back at the floor and began to walk away. I was alone. I was putting up protective walls in order to keep myself safe from the emotional pain I felt. I was sure there wouldn't be any rescue this time. I didn't get far before a car pulled alongside me. It was Ali, who had waited patiently outside for me to come out. He rolled down a window and asked me whether I would like a lift home. I couldn't speak. He coaxed me into the car and we went for a drive. It took me quite some time to talk to him, but his patience eventually settled me down and I began to relax. It took some time before I could tell him what had happened, either in the house or on the mountain.

Back at my house I became a recluse. I still hated being alone and I was happier when there was someone else in the house, but there didn't seem to be anything I could say. If I walked anywhere, my eyes never looked beyond my feet: I was very withdrawn. I lost sight of what I had achieved and of all the things I still wanted to do. I couldn't see the point and even stopped eating. That was when my friends, Sue, Fuzz, Carla and Ali decided that things had to change. They made me eat. Ali began to stay late, working with me or reading quietly so that I wouldn't be left alone. Slowly I began the long journey back. It wasn't easy. Any small thing could send me back to the mountainside – a careless phrase, the smell of damp soil, a cool breeze – and I would have to start all over again. One evening I began to write it down, to try to create a narrative of what had happened. It started as a letter to myself, typed into my computer but it became much more.

Much of that day was still carved into my memory. The smells and the path we followed. The things we said to each other, and as I wrote them down more came back. The memories were not in order by any means, but my first breakthrough was remembering my second, whispered, apology as I fell off the rock. It was for pushing myself too far and testing my limits to beyond the breaking point. I recognised the warning signs in my own behaviour and in Mike's as I went back through that day.

Pete was another great help for me. He was at University in Northampton, not very far away. He was always at the end of a phone and would call me two or three times a week. Because of our time at camp he knew me at my best and it was important for me to keep hold of that feeling. He came to visit and took me for another swim. This time I was determined to do better. Pete is a swimming teacher and I felt that I needed to be re-taught how to swim. He took me back through the basics of the strokes and the one I was most able to do successfully was backstroke. I wanted to swim front crawl but I just couldn't manage the breathing. My head did not turn, nor could I lift it up. I swam three lengths, and it took nearly an hour.

In my third week back I decided that I needed a better way to get around. Walking was just too slow and it was taking too long to get anywhere. I moved my bike out of the shed. After some puzzling about it I found that I could adapt to riding it. I couldn't sit on the saddle so I needed to stand on the pedals. I could only really use my left leg, so that meant another adaptation. I had pedals with straps that would hold my feet in so I developed a method of riding in which all the effort came from the left leg, pushing down and then lifting against the strap, while I stood on the pedals and leant the seat in against my left thigh. It's hard to describe, but it worked. This meant that I could now go further and faster than at any time since my fall. Freedom and independence were coming back into my reach. My normal high speed travel was still out of reach but I could go home between lectures and I was never quite as tired. I also took a first trip to the nearby supermarket, on my own, carrying my own shopping back. These are small milestones but they were very important for me.

When the canoe club met for their pool session in the third week of the semester, I pushed my luck and got into a kayak. Ali and another paddler anxiously held my boat for me as I eased my way slowly in. I was surprised to find that it felt alien. This was a shock. I tried to paddle it, but it felt odd. My body no longer moved as it once had. Strokes and movements that were natural to me the first time I was shown them were difficult or even impossible. I was horrified. This was my natural environment. If I couldn't paddle I would lose a very important part of my life. I had to think about what I was doing. The water felt heavy, like glue around me. Rotating my hands and body were unnatural movements. The boat had lost its supple, manoeuvrable grace and felt like a bathtub. Even sitting in the right position was uncomfortable. I was nervous about capsizing. I didn't want to show this to the club. I had finished the previous year as the most knowledgeable and experienced paddler in the club and now I couldn't sit in a boat properly. I had to really remind myself it was still an achievement; another step towards my recovery. As I struggled to get out of the boat on the side of the pool, it felt as if I had a lot further to go than I first imagined.

There wasn't a real long term plan. The overall goal was to get my life back to where it had been before the fall. This might not have been entirely possible; an overall plan would have looked unachievable, so I picked out small goals that were just out of reach. Each time I achieved one I looked around me and set the next. I had marker points and I used time with every one of them. I set out to reduce the time it would take every time I went anywhere. I was only competing with myself but every victory was a step towards recovery. I didn't know that I could never have the same life, but at the time it was all I dreamed of achieving.

For most of the areas in my life these small steps brought me satisfaction. Canoeing was the most difficult area. Everything had come so naturally to me when I learnt to paddle. I had never really had to try hard, even in getting through to the Student World Championships I hadn't trained hard. I had fitness and a natural ability on the water that had propelled me through all of the challenges so far. My difficulties must have been obvious. I went to every pool session I could, but when I got into the boat I began to experience nervousness and must have looked awkward as I tried to relearn the way in which I needed to move and flex my body to control the boat. Even now I can't remember how I did some of the moves before my accident. I had to completely relearn. I began to draw nervous looks from some of the other coaches. There were awkward silences and then, when I tried to help a new paddler with a stroke, two of them intervened and asked me to stop coaching. I was furious. There was a bit of a divide between those who were running the club. Most of my friends had left the previous year and I was on the wrong side of the divide. They were nervous that I was a risk to both myself and others on the water. It wasn't my paddling ability or knowledge, but fear of me doing further damage to my neck.

I struggled to cope with this. I was determined to sort things out, but my planned discussion turned into an argument fairly quickly. Two of us had a blazing row that became quite personal before I stormed out. At least this time I had a means of venting my frustration and aggression. I got onto my bike and began to ride it as hard as my adapted style would let me. I rode home and, insufficiently vented, rode it up and down the street outside my house, turning at a roundabout. On one of my laps I passed Sally and when I returned she jumped out and stopped me.

"What on earth are you doing?"

I was very upset as I explained what had happened at the pool session, and calming me down delayed her night out for quite a while.

It was a major blow. Canoeing was such an important part of my life; it represents who I am and I felt that I could no longer paddle with the University Canoe Club. More than that, their attitude challenged my own confidence in my ability to paddle. If they were right, my injuries made me a problem on the water and I would never be able to put myself or others at risk again. I was completely bereft. I stopped paddling, went back to not sleeping and trying to sort out my feelings with my journal.

Paul Anderson, from my home canoe club, came to my rescue. He was a part-time student at the time and therefore eligible to compete in the BUSA Wild Water Racing Championship. He heard that I wouldn't be there with the University Canoe Club and sent Bartman, his paddling partner, to collect me. I went to watch and support Paul. It was very frustrating and I left feeling very low. It reminded me of just how much I loved being on the water. Before I could do it I had a lot more recovering to do.

I concentrated on my small goals and my degree. I stayed out of canoes and kayaks. I didn't feel part of the club anymore, but there was lots more I could do. I found a way to make every journey a recovery exercise. I walked, rode and swam, pushing myself to go further and faster each time. In November I sent a triumphant MSN message to my friends, to let them know that I had run back from the supermarket for the first time. It might only have been 150 yards but it was a triumph. My friends celebrated with me. I can't overestimate the help that their attitude was. In a sport oriented University, on a course where the majority of students are constantly engaged in high level competitions, I had friends who would celebrate the smallest of achievements.

A few weeks later I found a lump on my head. I hadn't bumped it and it worried me. Apart from the usual worries that finding a lump causes, I was concerned that it could be connected to my head or spinal injuries. I made my first ever appointment with one of the university doctors. She felt it carefully and reassured me that it was just some fluid and nothing to worry about.

"Why did it bother you so much?" She asked.

"Well, the reason why I'm worried about it is that I had a sort of accident." I mumbled my response to her.

"What happened there?"

"Have you not had my notes?"

"No."

"Well, I fell off a mountain."

She sat back in her chair, "OK, tell me a bit more, what did you do?"

"I broke my neck, and my pelvis."

She put her pen down and looked at me closely. "And when was this?"

"Just before term started."

"This term?"

"Yes."

She gave me a thorough examination. All there was to show was my scars, each of which came with an explanation of how it had been caused and what had been done about it in the hospital. There was nothing she could do for my body, but she had a lot of experience dealing with damaged students, and had picked up that there were more issues I really hadn't dealt with.

"Would you like to talk to someone about it?"

My automatic response came out in a flurry, "I don't want pills!" I had an irrational fear that I would be given drugs and I didn't want them.

"No, there are people you can talk to about this. You

could go to one of the counsellors here to have a chat and see how you get on. You can come back to me in a couple of weeks to let me know how you get on."

I went straight to the counsellor's office to book an appointment. I'm very much a woman of action and there was no point delaying. I was very sceptical, though. My last experience with this kind of therapy had been at school and that didn't come out well. But I really needed the help. I had trouble concentrating and sleeping and both were affecting my work. The first appointment didn't seem to achieve much. In the hour that was available I explained what had happened to me and that was all we had time for. I simply rolled off the key facts and injuries, leaving any emotion out of it. The counsellor booked me in for a second session a week later. I don't like to let people down, so when the time came I went back, much to her surprise. My negative attitude at the first meeting must have communicated itself.

"I have to say," she told me, "that after you left I remembered that I had seen something in the paper about a student falling in America, so I looked it up. It was you, wasn't it?"

I hadn't realised that there had been media coverage that reached the UK. I remembered telling the doctors that I didn't want to talk to the press and they had kept it all away from me. She was interested in why I didn't want the news known. I finally admitted that it was because I was embarrassed by having fallen off a mountain. We began to explore why I was embarrassed and I left the session feeling, for the first time, that things were going to get better. I talked to her about my having written down bits of my experience, she encouraged me to do more, but it took a little while.

We kept talking for the rest of the academic year and I began to get a grip on what happened to me, and when. My counsellor intervened with my tutors, getting me the help and consideration with my marks and exams that I so badly needed, but was so reluctant to ask for. She helped me to develop strategies to overcome my worries and deal with the people around me. My drive to recover quickly, to lose the external signs of my accident had helped me to make a physical recovery; sadly it had actually hindered my mental one. It was my counsellor who began the process of healing me mentally and without both parts of this process I could never have achieved the things I have done since. I began to get some confidence back.

Things began to improve. I still struggled with my concentration and there were exams coming up at the end of February, but the Christmas break gave me a welcome holiday. I met up with my friends from Chelmsford Canoe Club for their Christmas night out. Paul took me aside and sat me down. He had been shocked by the Gilly he had seen at the BUSA Wild Water Championships. We talked about things I might do, and he promised me his support. Over the years he had become a father figure for me and his support was really important. He joined forces with Zoey, and they took me paddling. It rekindled my love of paddling. To follow it up he offered me a trip to Germany in April for the pre World Championship practices sessions. I promised to think about it. Back at University I threw myself into my studying. My room became study central and either Sharon or Ali seemed to be constantly there working with me. With the exams over we had a week's break. I needed a rest so Mum arranged for Tim, her, Josh and I to go to a Center Parcs resort near Nottingham. They collected me on their way up. In the peace of the traffic free holiday village, with constant access to a swimming pool I was able to relax. Mum could see that I was still having trouble mentally and she encouraged me to find a counsellor. For some reason I didn't want to tell her that I had already started. As the week went by I began to get the urge to write. It grew stronger and stronger. They dropped me back in my student house on the Friday afternoon and within an hour

I was in my room, writing. I worked almost non-stop and by Monday morning I had finished. I clicked the print button and watched as a thick pile of thirty sheets stacked up. I felt much better, but I had no idea what to do with it. I picked it up and held it out in my hands, as if offering it to someone, but no-one came to mind. I spent an hour just holding onto it.

I had a counselling session soon afterwards. I sat on the couch, feeling the comfort and repeating:

"I did it. It's all there. In one piece. I fitted the jigsaw together." I held my hands out in front of me, as if I was still holding onto the sheets of paper. My counsellor didn't need to ask what. She knew.

"Would you like me to read it?"

"I want someone to read it." I replied, "I just don't know who." It was so important, so personal, that I couldn't bring myself to give it to anyone yet.

Eventually I made my mind up. Sue was the newest of my housemates but we had become very close. I gave it to her. She took it upstairs to read. When she had finished she came down and gave me a big, long hug. No words were needed. A week after that I shared it with Sharon and Cara; they had been my two strongest supporters. Once again their response was to give me a big, long hug. It was what I needed. I was much more content after that and began to sleep and eat again.

I was growing in confidence, but not paddling was still a problem for me. The canoe club wasn't going to be a good outlet so I looked for something else. There was a coach training course coming up on the River Dart and I booked myself on to it. The Dart was where I first encountered white water and it has a special place in my affections. Before going I braved a pool session with Ali and practiced my rescues. So much was coming back, and knowing that I could still keep people safe was important for me before I went. The course was just what I needed. At that time coaches needed to be trained to level three before taking on the training of people on white water. Ali came with me and supported me throughout the weekend. On the first day I was a little tentative. I was suffering from nerves because I was in a boat, unsure of my personal skills and on moving water for the first time since my fall. It was also a definite test. The leaders of my university club thought I was unsafe. If the coach running the training felt I was unsafe then the club were right. As the weekend passed I gained more and more confidence. I could still do anything the trainer asked of me. My personal skills came back and my nerves slowly slipped away. At the final debrief he asked me a number of questions about my paddling.

I can't work you out," he said. "You are clearly a very experienced paddler, but you seemed to lack confidence. It's grown at an incredible rate. Don't know how to advise you about when to go for assessment."

It was time to come clean about by my accident.

"I wish you'd told me that before we started," he told me. "I'd have treated you differently."

"That's why I didn't tell you. I don't want to be treated differently." It was more than that. I needed someone who didn't know me, my history, or about the controversy over my safety to pass judgement on my paddling.

"I don't see you as a danger," he said. "You were the best paddler here. Just keep paddling."

It gave me the confirmation I desperately needed. I would keep paddling, and I would turn around the opinions of the Canoe Club. It didn't take long to come to a head. The coach who had taken the lead wasn't pleased to see me back. He immediately went for advice about my fitness to paddle and coach from the Student Union. They advised us to hold a committee meeting to try to resolve the issue. Ali came to support me and waited his moment while my detractor made his case. He savoured his moment as he pointed out that I was now the most qualified and experienced coach the club had. There was a shocked pause. This was news to them. He took his time. As a level three coach I was ahead of anyone else, my recent gaining of the qualification showed that a top level coach had worked with me and not found me to be a risk. Being accepted back was a very important point for me. I celebrated by taking up Paul's offer to paddle with him and Carl in Germany.

There was a pre-World Championship training event in Garmich-Partinkerkin, Germany. Paul had asked me to come to get me back into a boat and into the paddling he knew I loved. He may also have wanted to keep an eye on me and reassure himself that I was fine. It was my second time back on moving water since my fall and it was very different to the Dart. The waves were much bigger and the paddling much more committing and technical. I got back in a wavehopper, a plastic version of my river racer. I was scared but paddled on my instincts, which is when I am paddling at my best, after a few runs I began to find my groove. I loved it. Carl took up the position he had taken so often when I was learning, watching my back. I paddled on an ice melted filled river that is renowned amongst the racing fraternity as one of the most technically challenging race courses. I rolled and hand rolled the wavehopper, I was pleased and shocked at how easily I came back to autonomously paddling white water; my confidence came surging back.

It was a good way to go into my finals. I was very focussed. My room became study central again, with a stream of friends coming in to study with me. I was absolutely locked onto one goal, gaining a first class degree. I knew it was in my reach, but I would have to work for it. I worked so hard at revising that nothing else mattered or seemed important, that included eating. Once again, my friends were very good and picked up on this, making sure that we all ate together. In return I created an atmosphere in which we all gained better results than we might otherwise have done.

The exams flew past. My concentration was back and I was sleeping again. I went into my last exam ready to work for ninety minutes of hard maths and was totally focused on the task. I was extremely well prepared, and found that I had completed the work in less than half an hour. I went through it and checked it, then did it again. I was confident that I had got every question right and that there was nothing more I could do to improve my chances. I did something I have never done before. I walked out. I sat on the concrete outside and took some time to look back. I looked up at the sky and reflected. It was very quiet and peaceful outside of the exam hall and I took full advantage of it. I had arrived to start the year physically and mentally unready for it. All I had going for me was my determination to get my life back. In eight months I had gone from being someone who couldn't look after herself, walk unaided or sleep to a reasonably confident happy woman. I had learned how to heal both my body and my mind, and I had undertaken challenges that forced the people around me to accept me back as one of them. Everything had dropped back into place and my life was almost back to where it had been before the fall. When my friends came out there were some who were afraid that I had lost my focus and failed the exam, but I was confident. We went out and celebrated. It seemed that the whole university was partying that night. We were all desperate to ensure that we wouldn't lose the connections we had made. I was due to leave the next day to travel back to Camp Weequahic and found myself making two promises. The first was that there would be no dramatic events this time, a promise I was keen to keep. The second was that I would fly back for graduation in a few short weeks.

The next day brought lots more tears as I packed away the room that I had fought so hard in and made my farewells to my housemates and closest friends. I flew straight out to America. I was due, this time, to help with the pre-camp set up. As a three year veteran I was a senior member of the counsellor team. I had no bunk responsibility and was looking forward to taking up my old position on the waterfront team. This last visit was less enjoyable than the previous two. Many people knew about my fall, and it felt as if I was less trusted as a result. It might not have been true, but for me it overshadowed the trip. Early on a new counsellor from New Mexico had asked if anyone knew about the counsellor from Weequahic who had fallen the previous year. The room went uncomfortably quiet as people looked at me. My experience seemed to have matured me; I was no longer the girl who was sat in the same bunk the year before. Many child comforts, memories and safe places had been destroyed.

On this visit my friends were drawn from the older team members, those who had more life experience. I struggled to connect with team members of my own age, even those that I had known all three years I was there. I wasn't a kid any longer. The news that I had achieved my first class degree was welcomed, and I loved the trip back to graduate. For the rest of the time, it seemed more like a job than the wonderful experience it had been before and I was happy to be allowed to leave early. I jumped straight on a plane to Albuquerque and the girls met me at the airport.

They had split up to find me quickly. I ran into Kim first. She was delighted to see me and immediately phoned the others. They dashed over with a lot of excited squealing. The last any of them had seen of me I was being wheeled into the airport in a wheelchair and now I was back, almost completely restored, complete with backpack and paddle. They couldn't believe it. Despite our constant contact through the year they really hadn't expected me to look so well. They got me to jump up and down just to prove to them I could. I was the happiest I had been since before the fall. In Sam's apartment I felt as if I was home as they mothered and spoiled me. When I had left the previous year a big part of me had stayed and for the first time in a year I felt properly safe. Ali joined us a few days later and fitted in very well. We went back up the Sandia Mountain, but there was no question of them allowing me to walk anywhere on it without them. Sam drove us up to the top using the ski resort's road around the back of the mountain. I was just delighted to get to the top. Sam took my picture to prove it.

I spent a lot of time just looking at the slopes below me, I couldn't stop staring down. The mountain consumed my mind and I had to be dragged away from the edge where I was sitting. I was searching for where I fell but I couldn't find it. I looked for where I finally stopped tumbling but I couldn't see where that was either. Because I had spent so many hours staring at the top during my long night on the mountain, I thought it would have been easier to find from the top. It was like looking for a needle in a haystack amongst the bushes, trees and small canyons. In my mind I was trying to still pull all of the pieces of that night together in order to complete the jigsaw. This was one very important part of it and I had been unsuccessful. I went back into quiet Gilly mode. The girls didn't let me stay in this mode for long and soon got me smiling, their enthusiasm for life was just too infectious.

My stay there was like being a mini celebrity. We had all become so close during my short stay in hospital that I was taken to visit the girls' families and friends. Even being shown off as the Girl who had fallen and made the miraculous recovery didn't bother me. This had been the treatment I was afraid of in the UK, but somehow the closeness of our relationship made it an enjoyable experience. There was no chance of them leaving me alone, and even less of being allowed to walk anywhere unsupervised.

On the anniversary of the fall Kim, Jen, Ali and I took

a cable car ride back up the mountain. It was almost sunset. I had been a nightmare, reliving the day I had the year before. As we waited to go I had a strong feeling that this was the time I fell. We travelled up together in silence. At the top we watched the sun set and silently took the next tram car back down. On the way up we had filmed the view and I identified where I had been when I fell and where I landed. Ali was astounded, seeing the place and the actual height of the fall made a huge difference to his understanding of what had happened. Even though the place I identified from the tram was a long way away, you could still see the height. It was a teary time; and when Sam came home from work we all started again. None of us really wanted to, but we all were reliving the day.

When the time came, a couple of days later, to go home, I was inconsolable. I really didn't want to leave. Somehow the town of my worst experience felt more like home than my own country. I called one of the girls at every flight change. I had come a long way since the day of my fall. I was healthy now and my body seemed to be fully recovered. Mentally I had overcome some huge obstacles and things were looking better than they ever had before. It was also clear that I also had more to do. I needed direction and a purpose. I still wasn't confident in myself; it had been reduced, but the mountain still cast a shadow over me.

On the last, longest leg, I managed to find some composure. I had to continue living and not dwell too much on the past. Just before leaving camp I had heard of, and applied for a PhD opportunity back at Loughborough. I had an interview and needed to be ready for new challenges and a new future.

# 13 IN PURSUIT OF EXCELLENCE

I was walking with Ali along the Grand Union Canal in Loughborough when I came across the University Canoe Club again. Term hadn't quite started but the returning club leaders were out for a paddle, I was settling into a new house and my new PhD workload. They were surprised to see me back. We hadn't paddled much together in the past year but I was determined that I wouldn't be holding back on paddling in this year. The make-up of a University Club changes every year, and they were much more welcoming. It wouldn't have mattered if they weren't; I was going to paddle a lot more.

Things were already good. Although it was strange to be back at University without the friends who had sustained me for three years, it was just a symptom of the new start that I needed. I was being sponsored by Adidas to research into training shoes. It was a superb opportunity – sports industry experience with one of the sport's best known brands – and it used both my sports and my maths strengths. I had made two new friends, both American PhD students. It gave the place a transcontinental feel that connected me to my friends from Albuquerque and Weequahic and made me very comfortable.

I rejoined the Canoe Club with the new students. I still had some friends there: Nic, who had dislocated her hip the previous year and her roommate, Jo who was a sprint paddler started training with me. Jo gave me a kick start by sharing her sprint training plans with me. We trained together through the winter and she became something of a project for me. She had been paddling sprint for a long time, all of her family were involved with it and she was losing interest. To give them something to look forward to I introduced the two of them to Wild Water Racing. They took to it readily and spread their enthusiasm.

That year I took fourteen paddlers to the Dee for the BUSA Wild Water Racing Championships in Llangollen. It was the first time we had done anything like it. Up to this point competition had been seen as alien to the club's white water paddlers, but I started something new off. None of the fourteen paddlers thought they could manage something as challenging as that run, with two Grade IV rapids, but I made it fun for them, and by the time we came home we had all done it successfully and I had the start of a racing group. Nic, Jo and I entered the team race together, to see how they liked it. We paddled plastic river running boats which weren't as fast as racing boats, but gave the others a safer feeling. As we arrived at Town Falls, the Grade IV rapid that finishes the run I discovered that Nic has a form of Tourette's when things get harder. She swore at me loudly the whole way down, which made me laugh a lot. There was a big audience on the bridge as we passed under it and many of them were laughing. At the bottom I checked that they were fine and when we got to the end we had formed a strong team.

Before this the club's attitude to paddling had been that it had to be for pleasure. Words like training were treated as swearing. I showed them that there are many different kinds of fun to be had on the river and that competitions could be fun. It was the start of a major change of approach. I strongly believe that whatever discipline you choose, paddling is just paddling. It should be fun, even when you are taking it seriously.

As a group we began training on the local canal, working hard to get fitter, taking life in small goals. It went from strength to strength. We did polo, slalom and any other competition we could get into. It brought a new freshness into the club and its paddling. At one slalom competition every member of the team gained promotion from Division 4 to Division 3. I began to enjoy competing again. Prior to my fall I had always been nervous when competing, but the team atmosphere we created made it all much more enjoyable. I didn't realise it at the time but my mission to go back to international competition started here.

There was one small problem. As I began to paddle more I found that I grew uncomfortable increasingly quickly. I took a trip back to see Professor Dowell for an MRI scan of my back. It showed that my lower back was dislocated. The Professor put it down to my recovery. Pushing myself to get better quickly I had been rotating my hips and leading everything with my left leg to protect my pelvis. That had put a lot of pressure on my spine. It got to the point where I couldn't sit, stand or get into a boat for very long. Fortunately it was diagnosed as a problem that could be addressed by a physio. Most physios were unlikely to take me because of my still fresh neck injuries, but Professor Dowell was able to refer me to a specialist back physio. Gill Gillespie called me just over a week later to ask me in for a consultation. She wanted to check me out, look at my back and make a decision about whether she could treat me.

I was very nervous. I had just made it back into sport and now there was another decision in the hands of someone else, which would govern my future. I went all the way back to rock bottom. By co-incidence, Gill practices in Witham, the town that Mum lived in. We had never noticed the practice before. Mum came with me for moral support. I went in nervously with a big pack of x-rays and scans. She took them from me and threw them on the desk.

"I don't want to know about them. I want to know about you. Take a seat. What happened?"

"I broke my neck, and my...."

"I don't want to know about that. Tell me what the problem is."

"I can't sit in my boat?"

"Ok."

"And I'm struggling to sit and stand and it's really painful."

I liked her immediately. She was focussed on how my injuries impacted my life, not what they were. She has been a very valuable member of my team ever since that day, helping to put me back together whenever I do too much. We spent an hour talking. Half way through she made me stand and took a look at my spine. She walked around me carefully and then pulled out a skeleton.

"You hurt yourself here and here." She pointed at my neck and pelvis. "But you're hurting here. From my conversation with Professor Dowell the reason why you're hurting there," she pointed at the base of my spine, "is that your body's out of alignment. Have you noticed that your shoulders are two different heights?"

"No."

"Take a look at yourself in the mirror." She turned a full length mirror towards me. "Your knees aren't the same level, either." I loved the Biomechanics part of my degree so it all made sense to me. It felt as if she knew that this was the best way to talk to me. "We need to find out why this part is hurting." She made me walk up and down and eventually decided that it was all down to my feet. The way that I had adapted to my injury had significantly changed my gait and that had caused the pain and problems elsewhere in my body. I was fascinated.

This was what I was starting to study in my PhD. She experimented with some wedges under my feet and the pain immediately eased.

"I need you to get this fixed before we start," she told me. "I can refer you to a friend of mine, Craig Wilson, who makes orthotics locally. If you're lucky you might be able to see him today. After you've done a couple of weeks with the orthotics, come back and see me and we can start some physiotherapy. There's no point me starting work on you until you have a solid foundation to work from. Your pain would recur in about three steps from leaving here." I liked her ethos, that she was sorting the cause out first. I managed to get an appointment with Craig the same day. He agreed with Gill and showed me more about how my pelvis was affecting my position. He cast my feet and we made an appointment to collect them a week later. He warned me that my balance point would change as I settled into the way they would change my posture. He asked me about my PhD and then went into much more detail, knowing that I would be interested. My sports science background meant that I could quickly understand what he calls the "dark art" of orthotics. It was the start of a very fruitful relationship and I eventually became his roaming consultant.

After Christmas I was able to start physiotherapy with Gill. I had to travel for two and a half hours each way, between Loughborough and Essex, but it was worth it. Initially I saw her every week, but as she worked her magic it became every three weeks. She also suggested that I speak to her son, Adam, an injury specialist. Gill could see that my co-ordination was out and that my spatial awareness was poor. She was doing such a good job on my back that I decided it would be good for me.

Adam Gillespie is a personal trainer who works principally with people who are recovering from injury. He had me sit on a gym ball. I had no balance or core stability. My injuries had sapped the strength from all of the muscles in my pelvic region. For me to hold my back in the right way I needed to build them back up. He asked me to circle the ball with my hips and I couldn't. He moved me to a bench and asked me to lie straight. I couldn't. Worse than that I couldn't tell when I was straight and when I wasn't. Adam brought Gill back in to help. They must have spent hours with me that day, working out what was wrong. All the ways I had found to make my body work in the early days of recovery had created unnatural movement patterns and they were creating overuse and misuse injuries in other parts of my body. Working together Gill and Adam began to give me exercises to help me strengthen my body and rebuild my core strength.

I had also lost the co-ordination to carry out some of these movements. When they asked me to circle my leg I took nearly twenty minutes to work out how to do it. This seemed like a long time to all of us. Eventually Gill and Adam worked out that the narrowing of my spine had reduced my autonomy and caused problems with my co-ordination. I was going to have to pre-plan how to execute combined movements. In my early stages of recovery it was what I had done for individual ones. In my mind, I needed to think to turn what felt like one step backwards and actually see it is as sideways leap. It took me a while to see it like that, Adam and Gill were very good in encouraging me and were always honest in grounding my expectations. They were the ones who made me realise I was no longer the norm of the population and I would have to accept my differences. Over the years I have come to have a very close relationship with Gill. Eventually her work meant that I no longer needed regular appointments, but whenever my back gives me trouble, or my body stops co-operating, which it does from time to time, she is there to help me pull it all together again. I always follow her instructions.

Gill is very bubbly and eccentric. She loves to learn

and to educate the people she works with. She always looks for causes and fixes them ahead of carrying out physiotherapy. She's a fantastic listener and is someone I can always turn to when things aren't working well. She gives me the confidence to perform in sport. In 2009, when my back was giving me major problems we had a serious conversation. It was Gill who had the courage to tell me that paddling white water in my racer was accelerating problems for my back. The dynamic and fast reaction times needed to adapt the paddle in the waves and the power required was putting a lot of strain onto the whole of my neck region. It was one of the hardest conversations I have had with her. For any athlete the realisation that your days are numbered and what you love to do is now potentially affecting you long term sends you into turmoil. You question yourself on every aspect, could you have done something differently in the hope you find an answer that you can live with to confirm you did.

Gill is the one person who is able to sit me down and tell me off, forcing me to find different ways of achieving my goals. She uses Adam as an example. An ankle injury ended his professional football career and Gill helped him to find new outlets for his passion for sport. I was not ready to stop so I weighed up the risks and with her inspiration I went out and found a strength and conditioning coach who helped me build the muscles in my neck and she recognised his work. She loves the challenge of sorting my back out whenever I overdo things. Because I have had to deal with extreme pain my body is very good at blocking it out. Consequently I don't always recognise when I need to stop and she has helped me build up ways of recognising the signs.

Over the next six months I made massive improvements. Between Craig's orthotics and Gill and Adam's treatments they had worked miracles. I was back in a boat two weeks after starting therapy, on the Frostbite Tour, running interesting rapids with Adrian, Paul and Carl in Scotland. My body got stronger and better in every way.

Whenever I came up with new, more difficult goals, neither Gill nor Professor Dowell ever told me that I couldn't or shouldn't try for it. Their invariable response was "Let's find a way." Without them I could never have achieved so much. From March onwards I was constantly in a boat. I entered the BUSA Canoe Polo Championships with the university. Canoe Polo is a very high intensity sport. Halves are short, only six minutes each, but play is very fast and highly physical. I paddled with the university in slalom competitions, I trained daily on the river or canal and was building muscle in a way that Gill could feel on my visits.

Late in 2004 I told Gill that I wanted to compete in Wild Water Racing internationally. She gave me a long look and then said "OK, let's do it." It was typical of her attitude. Adam gave me a gym program to help me build up the strength I would need. Despite my sports science degree I had never been in a gym before. He took me through what I would need to do and then I joined my first gym in Loughborough. I saw him six weeks later and he measured my results. The muscle was holding my spine in place much better which meant much less trouble.

Once again, when things looked as if they were going well, there was something I had missed. In the winter of 2004 I started racing with a more serious intent. My first race was on the River Tees. The last race of the weekend was a sprint. This should be 500m to 800m in length, compared to a classic which is generally more than 5km. With any new race course, I did what I had always done and took a walk with Carl to check out the start and finish. The start was fine. The finish was a different matter. I found that I couldn't get to the finish line. You had to climb up a rocky face, with your boat. Even though there were people on hand to help it looked difficult. Then there was a switchback of a track back to the road. I couldn't do it. I got half way along the switchback before collapsing with a panic attack. I had tears running down my face, the other racers and spectators that all knew me passed me with puzzlement. I wanted the world to suck me down a hole and hide me, so they couldn't see my fear. Carl sat me down to try to sort out the problem. My legs felt stuck in one place and for a while I couldn't move from that spot. My thoughts were racing: I could get into my boat, but how would I get out at the end? If I couldn't walk down to the finish, how would I ever walk from it back to the top? What would happen if I slipped on the rocks? Would I fall? There were too many questions and no answers. I was working myself into a never ending spiral.

By the time Carl had convinced me to walk down to the finish, the practice time had almost ended. I was gutted. I had let my fears get to me and shown someone else my weakness. I was used to hiding these things. My embarrassment was compounded by the age old question: 'what would other people think of me?' I felt a failure.

Carl tried to reinforce that it wasn't the water that I was afraid of. If I could have taken the rapid and put it somewhere else I would have competed. Time passed as I struggled and the races took place without me. At the end, I struggled to stand with my fellow competitors at the prize giving. I felt as if "Failure" was written across my forehead and did not feel I could stand beside them. I stewed in the car all the way home going over and over what had happened as I began my walk down the switchback. I couldn't explain it to myself. It felt completely irrational. After a few hours of silence, Carl proposed a solution. He had put some of the pieces of the puzzle together that I could not. I was associating the switchback with falling and this linked to the mountain. He proposed going back to the Sandia Mountains to face my fear where it began: in the foothills in Albuquerque, New Mexico.

Carl and I flew over at Christmas with my sister, Claire.

I only told Sam that I was going. I didn't want the girls to talk me out of walking on the mountain. I needed to do this in my own way and with the people I trusted most, I certainly had no trust in my own judgment or ability to make decisions since falling. The aim was to walk part of the route, to find out where we had gone wrong. We went into the foothills, walking from where we had started we found that we had gone wrong before we had ever reached the La Luz Trail. Knowing that helped me enormously. As ever for me, achieving one goal meant that it was immediately replaced with a new one: I wanted to go to the top. My walking pace increased and I became annoyed that Claire and Carl were not keeping up with me. Getting to the top was my new overriding goal: I thought by reaching the peak, it would provide me with the answers and my jigsaw would be complete. I would be able to move on with my life and stop being held back by being unable to answer what had happened that day in August. I thought it would stop me thinking about the fall in every waking and sleeping moment. It wasn't to be that day. Carl is an experienced walker who I have always trusted with my life and Claire was going to make sure I was safe, but it was winter and it really wasn't the right time. I knew I would be going back another time.

This was my second visit after the fall. We also visited the top, travelling up on the tram. Just as I had done on the previous visit I sat, searching for the spot where I had fallen. With snow on the ground it was very hard to see and I was getting frustrated at being unable to pinpoint it. Carl, however, was determined to make a negative place a positive one. I was deep in thought, staring at the vegetation below me, when I was thrown out of it by a blow to my head and a cold wet splattering of snow drops getting between my layers of clothes. I turned around and another snowball, thrown by my sister, hit my chest. There was only one response possible: a snow fight began, followed by some rolling and wrestling in the snow. By the end all three of us lay on the snow, breathing heavily and laughing. We spent the rest of our trip travelling and visited the Grand Canyon. Once again I didn't get to go right to the bottom so that is another challenge that I will have to complete.

We ended our trip in Las Vegas. The night before we were due to leave, Carl asked me what I really wanted to do. I didn't really have to think about it. I had been quietly considering it ever since talking to Gill about international competition, but hadn't wanted to put it into words.

"I want to go to the World Championships." These were due to be held in 2006, and Carl knew instinctively that I meant to try for selection to get onto the team in 2005, to gain experience at some World Cups. Selection was in April, only four months away. It wasn't going to be easy, a more sensible plan would have been to try for the following year, but sensible is for plan B. Carl didn't hesitate. He agreed to support me.

Once home I was completely focussed. We went to the Tryweryn nearly every weekend to train on white water. I was really driven. Behind my motivation was the wrong reason. Going back to Albuquerque had helped me to deal with my fall, but it had also brought back other memories, not least Mike telling me that the only way he could cope with his trauma was to tell himself that I had died on the mountain. I needed to prove to him and to myself that I wasn't just alive; I was as good as or even better than I had ever been. At weekends Carl was pretty much the only person I spent time with. He helped me find the best line down, encouraged and supported me. I was still having trouble with climbing banks after a race and he began to train me to deal with it, sending me up gradually steeper and higher banks until I could face anything the river threw at me.

In Loughborough I went in search of training partners. I contacted Soar Valley Canoe Club and found a group of very strong paddlers to train with. Jon Schofield, then a former Wild Water Racing Junior World Champion, later to be a bronze medallist at the London Olympics, was part of the group. He was training with Jessica Oughton, and Neil Blackman. We were all paddling Wild Water Racing boats and Jon and Jessica were the golden children. Both were top of the league in the sport. They pushed me hard, but not as hard as I was pushing myself. I knew that Jessica was going to be the girl to beat and I set myself the goal of becoming faster than her on flat water. I was training every single day, twice whenever I felt I could manage it. A typical week began with a training session on the canal, followed by a polo training session at the pool. Tuesday and Thursday I trained with Soar Valley, Wednesday was another day on the canal with anyone I could persuade out onto the water with me. Fridays were occasionally a rest day and on Saturday and Sunday I would be at the Tryweryn in Wales, doing as many runs down the river as I could fit in. I stopped taking my car and cycled or walked everywhere. I would have been running but it was still too much impact on my back and I found it the hardest thing to coordinate my body to do. Whenever I wasn't paddling or working I was in the gym, building my strength. It was working and Jessica was not pleased to find me hauling her in.

I made the selections in my best ever condition. My fitness was good and I knew that, even if I couldn't paddle faster than Jessica I knew the river and had better moving water skills than her. Mentally I was less well prepared. On my first practice run I got lost, forgetting all of the routes. I was terrified that I was there for the wrong reasons and would blow it. Carl, as ever, patiently picked up the pieces, forcing me to decide what I really wanted. I really wanted to represent my country. Before the race I spent over an hour with my head in my hands, trying to mentally prepare myself. When my turn came I knew the lines and worked hard but had no idea whether it was enough.

Two weeks later, while my sister was visiting, my phone rang.

"Hello?"

"Hi, Gilly, I'm ringing to let you know that you have been selected for..."

That was all the information I took in. I finished the call on autopilot and bounced through to the living room screaming with delight. Claire joined in enthusiastically. I was going to represent my country! It was my childhood dream. Eventually we calmed down enough for Claire to ask me what I would be doing. I wasn't sure. My mind was a blank after the word, selected. I had to call back and a very patient coach explained that I had been selected for the World Cup Series and more importantly, the European Championships. I was ecstatic. I hadn't dared hope I would be selected for the Europeans.

The World Cup Series was held in the UK and Ireland. The proudest moment for me was pulling on my GBR tracksuit. I didn't make a good start to the paddling. The pressure of paddling in a GBR vest got to me. It wasn't just race day, but for a whole fortnight before the race I was swallowed up by the thought of paddling for my country and not being good enough. I reached a realisation that I had been doing it for the wrong reasons. I didn't need to prove that I was alive to Mike or anyone else. I wanted to do it for myself. Somehow that realisation increased the pressure. In my first race, on the River Trent, I messed up the line and swam. I was devastated, it was the first time the whole of my family had come to see me paddle let alone race and I hadn't even reached the finish line. I felt I had let everyone down. I couldn't look them in the eyes. I thought I had 'failure' written across my forehead along with 'idiot'. I was wrapped in negativity. It was a friend, Rob, who was later to be a housemate, who persuaded me to see things differently. He helped me to face my family and once I did their response was the opposite of what I expected: they were just so proud of what I had done and were full of support. The next race was a few days later. Once again I spent a considerable amount of time sitting quietly getting my mindset right before I went back on the water. I didn't show any real paddling quality on that World Cup Tour, but it had the desired effect of getting me used to the level of competition. I did better in each race and my confidence grew with every outing.

Alan Tordoff, the head coach, was very impressed with my drive and passion, but worried about me burning myself out. He sat me down to talk through my training. For the first time I was given a training program, with clear sessions and goals. I followed it religiously, training less, but much more effectively. For the first time ever I reached a peak in my training just in time for the European Championships in France. I was absolutely flying, recording some very fast runs in training.

The setting for the European Championships was amazing. The River Chalaux was beautiful and demanding, but had just the kind of features that I felt I could excel on. My preparation went well; I learned the route and was more ready to perform than I had ever been. The first day was sprints and the whole site filed up with people. There were grandstand areas, camera men and even a big screen so that supporters could see the whole race.

I was very excited as I lined up for the first sprint, my anxiety was under control and I knew that if I kept my composure and kept paddling as I had been I was in for a good result. The countdown started and I positioned myself ready to go, then four beeps at one second intervals followed by a long one signalled that it was time to go. I felt supremely in control as I took my boat around the first obstacle and then, thirty seconds into the run I clipped a rock. I had just a little too much edge on my boat and it threw me over. I was irritated at the lost time, but it wasn't a disaster. I extended my arm and paddle to flip the boat up again and as I did so my shoulder hit a submerged rock. It hurt, but didn't stop me. I tried to move my paddle into the rolling position but it didn't respond properly. I took another attempt before realising that my arm was wiggling and loose in places it shouldn't be. I had dislocated my shoulder. I didn't want to accept that rolling wasn't going to happen. Taking a swim in a competition is embarrassing enough, but to do it at the start of the European Championships is much worse.

There seemed to be cameramen everywhere, capturing every moment and broadcasting it to the big screen at the finish. I didn't want to be seen swimming on it. I took one more try, relying much more on my hips to rotate the boat and managed to get it upright to the sound of loud applause. Below the water everything had slowed down, but on the surface I found that I had not travelled very far, maybe four metres, and had only been under for a few seconds. I was still at the top of the rapid and needed to be in control of my boat. Giving up now would mean that my boat and I would be swept down the rapid out of control, certainly going broadside onto rocks and breaking. With just one arm working I managed to get a stroke in and straighten the boat up, pointing back down the racing line. The sensible option would have been to find a good eddy and break out of the current. I don't always take the sensible option but the river would take me down a small rock slide and then I would have to find a route through the next rapid. I was torn: I was desperate to finish the race at all costs but I took the safer option and spun the boat in to the side. I could hear the public address system announcing my retirement.

My shoulder was hurting and I knew something serious was wrong. The best case was that I had dislocated it. I didn't want to think about the possibility of having damaged my spine. Without my arm working I couldn't even get out of the boat. I was stuck. I looked up the river for help and could see some first aiders. I waved to them. They looked down and one of them waved back. My French was hopeless; I didn't even know how to call them for help. I began to worry about communicating my problem if they did come down. Almost as I thought it, Carl turned up and hurried down the bank.

"What's wrong?"

"My shoulder, I think." As soon as I started talking I had to fight to hold back tears.

"It can't be dislocated, it would hurt a lot."

"Um, it does hurt..."

"Can you get out?"

"I don't think so."

He took his sandals off and slipped into the thigh deep water beside me to help me out. He pulled my deck and took me into a bear hug, lifting my body out and we toppled towards the bank. For a moment I lay there, on top of my friend, with one foot tucked into the cockpit of the boat to keep it from floating away to be pounded to pieces in the rapids. Suddenly we were surrounded by people all wanting to help. One took my boat. The first aiders started to look at my shoulder. We had communication difficulties immediately. They removed my buoyancy aid, inexpertly and painfully pulled my cag away and revealed a very obvious dislocation. They tied me an ineffective sling and brought a stretcher down. I wasn't thrilled. I didn't want to go on a stretcher in front of all these people. I shook my head and stood up. I would walk up the path.

I must have looked comical. I had canoe shoes, neoprene shorts, my spraydeck and my lucky sports bra on, that was all. The path was steep and not too difficult, but the pain brought back my fear of falling. Carl asked me whether I was sure I wanted to walk. If I had been in charge of this situation for another casualty I wouldn't have let them walk. There were far too many unknowns, not least being the chance of other injuries and shock.

Carl knew me well, though, and put his arm around me to help me walk. I was deeply upset. It wasn't so much the pain, but the loss of the dream. I had worked so hard to get to this point. I was feeling sorry for myself and wondering whether there was a message in this for me. The previous time that I had been in a position to represent my country; I had fallen from a mountain. Today I had dislocated my shoulder.

For a short while I stood in sight of the world, just below the big screen, and then I was led to a large red four by four. The journey off the site was long and bumpy. They drove slowly to keep the disruption to a minimum but it hurt a lot. At the top car park I was taken to a first aid tent where we waited for the ambulance. I knew that the less time my shoulder was out of place, the easier it would be to put it back, but no-one seemed willing to do it. Without a language in common I found it impossible to ask, so I resigned myself to a long wait with no pain relief. One of the team popped in to ask how I was.

"I'm smashing." What else can you say? I was devastated and hurting, but somehow this little line eased the dread I was beginning to feel about going back to hospital, it made me smile and helped me pass the time.

Carl followed the ambulance to a hospital and was by my side as soon as we arrived. There was nothing like the fuss I had experienced in America. My injury wasn't life threatening and we had to wait to be seen. It took hours. I began to shake with shock, and was troubled that I didn't seem to be able to handle this pain as well as I had handled the pain on the mountain. The only pain relief I had been able to take was aspirin and it wasn't doing anything. This time, however, I wasn't alone. Carl stayed with me and comforted me throughout my wait for treatment.

Eventually a doctor arrived. He examined me and decided that I needed an anaesthetic to relax me while they put my shoulder back in. I didn't want to be put to sleep. All the fears of the mountainside were back with me. If I slept I might never wake up. Carl did his best to reassure me that I would only be out for a couple of minutes, but it wasn't working. It was the calm, competent manner of the Anaesthetist that finally reassured me. I sometimes wonder about the psychology of what made me trust her. While I slept I dreamt that I was paddling the Etive, in Scotland. It's an adrenaline junkie's paradise; full of big drops that are relatively easy to do, if you can summon the courage. It was followed by a dream of a successful run down the Chalaux, the river that had just broken me. I was really enjoying it, and was put out to wake up before I had finished the run. I complained to Carl who had trouble explaining to me that I had been out for less than a minute. I was moved to a recovery ward for a few hours, high on anaesthetic and chattering away to Carl before being released.

Getting out of the hospital was the first challenge. I was still wearing my spray deck, and on top I now had an immobilising body wrap that just left the hand of my injured am free. We burst out laughing. We finally found the car. Carl started it up then paused and looked at me.

"Now we've got a problem. I don't know where we are, and we've got to find a hostel that's about fifty kilometres from nowhere."

It was the funniest thing I had ever heard and sustained us on the journey. When we finally got back I put a brave face on for the team. I didn't want to upset the juniors who were also there, but more than anything I didn't want anyone to know how devastated I was not to have raced. I spent the rest of the trip supporting the team from the bank, but I knew I had a lot of work to do to get back from this. However strong my body had become I needed to build up my metal reserves. I wanted that World Championship place the following year and I was determined that I would get it. Deep down I knew I could do it.

# 14 INTERNATIONAL DREAMS

Repairing a dislocated shoulder was much less worrying for me than a broken neck had been. I needed some rest to help it repair itself, so I threw myself into my work. I was invited to Japan to present a conference paper. It was my second visit to the Far East, but I was presenting my first published article which was very exciting. We added in some touring and factory visits in China. Just before flying out, and only two weeks after my dislocation I was on the Tryweryn, paddling plastic boats on the Lower, with my friend Jo. We took it easy, floating, talking and giggling as we did the entire four miles in about twenty paddle strokes. To help rebuild my confidence I also entered the National Canoe Sprint Regatta. I wasn't there to try to win, just enjoying being back on the start line and crossing the finish line.

I tried to not look at the dislocation as a setback: I reframed it as a slight inconvenience which slowed down my journey to my overall goal of the World Championship. A dislocation is not a minor injury to get over; it takes time to repair, physically and mentally. But repairing myself was something that I had experience of: my ability to push myself to my limit and my small goal technique, were two tried and tested techniques I had had great success with. It worked really well and it was not long before I was back to my usual routine. I didn't question my speed of physical recovery until I saw the amazed expressions of fellow competitors when they questioned me on the rumour that they had heard about me sustaining a serious injury. How could I be racing when I had just dislocated my shoulder 4 weeks ago? On the Gilly scale of injuries it was not serious.

It was the start of another university year. As a PhD student one year rolled into the next. This year I was elected as the Competitions Secretary for the University Canoe Club and wanted us to do well in every BUSA competition that year. The first event was Wild Water Racing on the River Washburn in Yorkshire. Just before term started I took a couple of the students to one of the National Division A races being held on the Washburn, so they could get used to the course. In hindsight I was a little naive. My shoulder was still recovering but it felt fine. I didn't know enough about the recovery process to be aware of the risk and to make things worse I had lost a lot muscle strength since the previous summer. But I loved being on white water too much; I was so desperate to get back to racing my boat on the rough that I overestimated what I could do.

Between race runs I met up with my old friend and former coach, Paul Anderson. He encouraged me to join him on some training runs in between the race runs, which I did. I underestimated the number of runs and how tired my body was getting. I had gone back to old habits of not wanting to show weakness and to please people. I was trying to prove to everyone that 'I was fine'. My learned ability to shelve and block my bodies warning signals was finely tuned. The pressure on my weak shoulder let me down on my next race, the classic run. I couldn't hold my boat in position and I capsized. My shoulder didn't have the strength left to allow me to roll and I took a swim. It was a disaster: I damaged my boat and reopened the wound on my leg. I was devastated and when I got my boat to the bank tears flowed down my cheeks. It was the realisation that I was not invincible and I could not get away with not listening to my body that upset me. I had to walk back along the side of the bank, passing parents, friends and partners of racers. I tried to pass them as if nothing was wrong at all, trying to smile through my sadness. Trying hugely to pretend there was nothing wrong. This is a little difficult when you have an open wound where you can see pure white bone. To protect myself, I had to pretend to myself it was not a problem and it was just another inconvenience. It was far more than that and deep down I knew it. After a visit to hospital for stitches one of the students had to drive me home. I sat quietly in the passenger seat, fighting back tears and depression.

I needed to take some time out to recover. It's something I have never been good at. Whenever I saw a boat, knowing that I had to rest and couldn't paddle, it triggered a wave of anger. I needed to be in a boat and couldn't. My boat on the water was my safe and sacred place. It was where my whole world made sense and I could forget my troubles. I tried to avoid paddle sessions and the canoe club but, as a committee member, I couldn't miss the Freshers' Bazaar. I was sulking around the back of the stand, sitting on the floor and trying to elevate a painful leg when one of the team came to fetch me.

"Gilly, we've got a girl here who is interested in racing and you're into the kind of long pointy boat paddling thing. Can you talk to her?"

"Oh, if I must," I sighed. I was not in the frame of mind to be excited and had little patience for talking to a beginner and I got up reluctantly. I was introduced to Kat Burbeck. It was one of those moments that could so easily have been missed. She was bubbly and very enthusiastic about racing boats. I had intended to move her on quickly, but we bonded instantly, spoke for at least half an hour, in the middle of which we somehow managed to agree that we would one day enter the Devises to Westminster Race together.

Student experiences of Paddlesport can be very sink or swim. Kat had some experience of paddling on flat water but none of white water. I knew that if I left her to the club she would be pushed quite hard to prepare her for the Student Championships in six weeks and I didn't want her to be put off by that. I took her quietly under my wing. It was good for me as well. It gave me something to focus on while my leg mended and kept me in touch with the sport, both at a practical level and with the University club. Kat's bubbly personality helped to open up my social horizons. Before long we were like sisters, everywhere we went it was "Kat and Gilly". It was a really good relationship that lasted well after we left the university. She was the first person I helped train to an international level. I set up training groups on the canal and we were joined by Heather Corrie, who was an international standard, and later Olympic, slalom paddler. I reconnected with my old training squad from Soar Valley and we built some strong cross club training sessions as Jon Schofield, Grant and others from the Slalom and Polo disciplines joined us. She had the right attitude and within a year she was ready to compete in the Student World Championships.

My main focus was the World Championships. I needed to compete enough to be eligible for selection, but not injure myself. Alan Tordoff supplied me with a base training program, and I set to work hard. I was still driving down to train with Soar Valley in Leicester and taking my university group out on the other days. As the winter passed we moved to a more direct program. Paul Anderson was also in touch and every Wednesday afternoon I would drive over to meet him in Huntingdon. We would go for a pizza and then go onto the river for an hour of very hard work, at the end of which I would usually feel as if I was going to throw up the pizza. Paul worked within the sessions I had been given by Alan Tordoff and personalised them to maximise my potential. After a while we discovered that I had a problem. At about thirteen minutes my heart rate would drop, and I would unconsciously put less effort in. Paddling alongside me, Paul could see that my boat was definitely slowing down. We analysed my performance closely and worked to find strategies to deal with it.

My pursuit of a World Championship goal became all consuming. I realised that it wasn't compatible with my PhD work and that if I wasn't careful one or both of them would suffer. I went to my tutors and discussed my options. We agreed that if I was selected I would be able to have a couple of months off. It wasn't easy. I also needed permission from adidas, as my sponsors, to shift the deadlines. It all dropped into place.

I began to focus my efforts on the Classic event. Covering four to five miles of Class II – IV white water was going to take about twenty minutes and was ideally suited to both my river reading skills and my endurance levels. We worked on splitting the twenty to twenty four minutes into segments, preparing me to maximise the effort I would be able to put in.

In the New Year I began to attend squad training weekends. This was all about the rough water, where to place strokes, how to read the water and fine tuning our technique to get our skills to the highest level. Some of the canoe sprint world class coaches became involved because they could see that we were becoming a strong team. By March we knew that the course was no longer going to be held in the UK, on the Tryweryn. The new location was the Czech Republic. We went out for a training weekend to get to know the course. There was snow on the ground and blocks of ice floating in the river when we arrived. The river wasn't unlike the river we had been training on. There was less rock, but it was still essential to find and be on the right line through shallow shingly rapids with strong and building wave chains. There were fewer manoeuvres required for most of the course, but at the end of it you ran through the town and were carried under hotels that had been built across the river. It also had a strange feature where the water rises over an obstruction, banks around a corner, and actually takes you up rather than just downstream. It was easier than it looked, but it was a strange experience to paddle. It looks like a huge, intimidating wall of water as you approach it and feels like a slide as you go over. It reminded me of the feelings you get on a helter-skelter. The very last features were a series of drop off weirs that required an accurate line to get just right. I paddled it as many times as I could in that weekend, trying to be sure of where the lines were.

I put everything I could into preparing myself. I followed my training plans, resting when I needed to, which is something that doesn't come naturally to me. I was having regular physiotherapy with Gill to keep my neck and shoulder strong. She was also working with me on my mental strength and self confidence, helping not to worry about my shoulder coming out again. I was sharing a house with Rob, a former Commonwealth rower. He helped me to think about my nutrition, planning my food to supply the energy and nutrition that I needed. For the first time, I realised, I was becoming an elite athlete. It was a new experience. The first time someone had described me as a Great Britain Athlete I was surprised. I almost denied it. But at long last I felt as if I belonged in the squad.

Selection was in Scotland, on the River Tay. The Classics were held at Grand Tully and on the River Awe. Kat, who had been joining me in races, came up with me to support me and ran along the banks shouting "Paddle" wherever she could. There was very strong competition that year. Tina Parsons had been the fastest paddler in this category for years. She had represented Britain four times in the past six events and had taken a Bronze Medal in the team event at her first World Championships. She was very fast on the flatter courses. Dee Paterson was close behind her; she had been the only Lady to make the team two years before. Jessica Oughton, in her first year as a senior, and I were the other main contenders. I wasn't sure that I had shown them enough quality.

At that time, there were three main events in each category at a World Championships. The Sprint, which tends to be about one to one and a half miles, and the Classic, which is about four to five miles long. Most attention is placed on the Sprint, but the Classic was more my taste, with an effort suited to my endurance. Last but not least is the Team Race. This uses the Classic course and requires a team to bring three boats down the course together. There is a particular skill required to assist the slower paddler by towing them in the wake behind the faster boats. In flat water racing this is known as wash hanging and can be a controversial tactic. In team racing, it's as essential as a peleton in cycling. It was my best chance of a medal in the World Championships and I wanted it badly. Jessica was still faster than me on flatter courses, but she knew how badly I wanted the place. We pushed each other very hard in the heats. The wait for the selections to be announced was especially hard. When it finally came it was frustrating. All four of us, together with Jenny Hyslop, who would only be competing in the sprint were selected. Only Dee and Tina were given places in the team event. They had been unable to decide between us and were leaving it until they saw how well we were paddling at the event.

I invoked my agreement with adidas and the University, and took a couple of months off so that I could step up my training, aiming to peak in time for the championships. Two weeks before the event we had a squad training event on the Tay. It lasted five days and was on similar water: flattish shingly rapids with reliable water levels. One of the most important factors was learning to paddle as a team. We ran the river in every conceivable combination, trying to get used to each other's paddling style and learning tactics for keeping the group together. At the end of the session they were no nearer to a decision than they had been before. Jessica was still a little faster than I was, but I really wanted the place.

My preparation complete, there was one more thing that needed to be done. I had been talking to Rob about my boats and the need to care for them. We compared them with running shoes that you could just pull on and forget, fitted properly they become an extension of you. Rob explained that in Rowing they tended to name boats, something we don't tend to do in canoeing, where the boat becomes more an extension of you than in other sports. I had three boats. One that Carl had given me, which was slightly more stable and I used for practice, another, a different design, was my first choice race boat. Rob offered to prepare them for me and took them away, to polish and prepare them. Then he invited me to a barbeque to wish me luck. He had arranged for a naming ceremony for my boats, having come up with names and produced the stickers for them. My practice boat became Bala Zapados, meaning Dancing Shoes. I loved the name. My race boat was called Lugar Feliz, meaning happy place. Both names were very apt. Whenever I'm in a racing boat I am definitely in my happy place. The third was Jaguaaar. Neither of us being drinkers, we christened them with Blackcurrant Squash. It was a very special moment. No-one else in the squad had named boats.

I arrived in Karlovy Vary very much ready to compete. I flew out with Jenny, who was becoming a very good friend. We arrived a week before the competition to give us time to practise the course and prepare. I had never been so fit. I was totally prepared, I knew the water, I was peaking both physically and mentally. As we drew nearer to the day more people began to turn up. I was sure I had seen Mum at the opening ceremony. She had come to see me race. She was very good, and left me alone so as not to increase the pressure.

I put my boat into the water for the classic, my first race, and settled into it. All too soon the paddler before me started, they called me forward and I arrived on the start line. Everyone has a full minute waiting and it's a horrible minute. You try to compose yourself, to visualise the water ahead. At fifteen seconds before you start you hear a single "boop". At five seconds it starts to boop on every second until the last long boop which means it's time to go. I have been known to crumble under the pressure of those five boops, but this time I had something Kat had said before I left to keep me strong.

"Gilly, I know you were really nervous last year, but just enjoy it. Think of it as no different to a national race. On that start line take one second to smile. Have an excited 'eek' moment. Remind yourself that you are at the World Championships and you made it there through your own achievements." It was what I needed. I was excited instead of nervous. The countdown ended and I put my paddle deep in the water, pushing my boat past it. I focussed my whole being into that run. Everything went exactly as I had planned and visualised. I knew what I had to do, and I could feel time ticking away by the second. I took the line I wanted down every rapid and put everything I had into each stroke. You run the race on your own and my focus was on my time. I had a target and I was absolutely determined to beat it. I knew what the effort required felt like and I worked hard to keep it there. Jenny was at the bottom to meet me, carrying a bottle of water. I could barely speak, and the only thing I wanted to know was whether I had made my time. She looked at the clock and began to jump up and down in excitement.

"You've done it, you've done it!"

Everyone seemed very excited. I had beaten my target time by about three seconds and at my first World Championships I was fifteenth in the world. I was very happy with the achievement. I had stopped worrying about how anyone else had paddled; my own performance was all I could affect. Around me my friends seemed to be almost too enthusiastic with their congratulations. It wasn't until a couple of hours later that one of the coaches told me the important thing that I had missed. I had beaten Jessica. The team race place was mine. I was ecstatic.

The next day were the sprints and I had to prepare myself to race once more and then again for the team race the following day. The team order was that Tina would lead, I would sit on her wash, our boats almost touching, and that Dee would follow behind on my wash. The idea is that a boat on a wash is pulled forward faster, slightly slowing down the boat in front. By putting the slowest paddler in the middle you can take 15 to 20 seconds off their fastest time. It went wrong from the start. We hadn't practiced this combination on the Tay and Tina was nervous of having me paddle so close. When you are running through white water a touch on your boat can push you off line and she was worried about it. She set off too fast and never slowed enough to pick me up. I didn't have a chance of getting onto her wake. Dee sat perfectly on my wake shouting instructions. I did my best and we still put in a fast run. When I looked at my watch it was almost as fast as I had done on my solo run, despite the drag of Dee's boat behind me. I didn't know where we had finished, but I was euphoric. I had finished my first World Championships and put in two of my best ever white water runs. We had to get off the water there and have our boats weighed so I could finally relax and I wandered around in a happy daze. By the time I had recovered both Dee and Tina had got back into their boats and set off for the get out, a mile down the river, without me.

I joined up with some Austrian and German girls who had finished their run. We had trouble communicating, but they were pleased to see me. They remembered my dislocated shoulder and congratulated me on making it back to international competition. We dawdled down the river together. I found a strange atmosphere in the British team. I was late in, and had lost the best part of an hour getting there. Most of the team was waiting to load our boats onto a trailer ready to leave for the World Cup Series the next day. Tina and Dee seemed subdued but most of the lads were congratulating me. I went to the coaches and told them that I had given everything I could on that run, and apologised that it hadn't been enough. The coaches knew that. They told me I had done well, but didn't seem to be saying that to the other two. We had completed the run in the same time as my individual run. If we had done it well we should have been able to go 15-20 seconds faster. The analysis began with a commentary of how the German's had done. I realised that we had been close to a medal. I began apologising again but they told me that it wasn't my fault. They didn't really explain until after the World Cups were over. It had been the way that my team mates had behaved that had cost us the time. A team working together pulls the slowest paddler faster along the course. We hadn't worked together. I was the slowest paddler and even though I had put everything I could into it, without full team cohesion, without trust in each other's ability in the boat, there was little chance that we could make the crucial seconds up. At the end of the day we just hadn't practiced paddling together enough.

That evening there was a huge athlete's party in an ancient castle. The alcohol flowed freely, but I have never needed it. My mother has a knack of getting on with new people and she had made friends with the Irish team who brought her in to the party. It was nice, once the pressure of racing was off to spend some time with my mother. She had also brought my brother in who, at the age of ten, was finding the drink fuelled antics of the athletes puzzling. I was delighted to be there, at the end of a World Championships, to have paddled the best I was capable of at the time and to have come fourth in the team race. Fourth in the world! I hadn't let myself or my country down. My body was holding up well. I could only get faster. This was just the start.

# 15 THE END OF THE DREAM

The first World Cup races started in Italy, in Val de Sol. I made a good start. I was learning both the Sprint and Classic courses and starting to feel that I could apply real power to the run. My confidence took a massive knock on the second training day when on the first run of the afternoon my paddle snapped in half. I was in the middle of a power stroke when the centre of the shaft gave way. I was unaware of it at the time, but I had a faulty shaft. As I pushed with my top hand and put weight onto the blade, with all the tension that was driving the boat forward, it broke in half. My whole body was driving forward against the blade and the momentum I had generated left me following it into the water. At that point I had no real idea of what had happened, just that my paddles didn't seem to be behaving right as I automatically tried to set up for a roll. With a half paddle in each hand it was no real surprise that I couldn't do it. I pulled my spraydeck and bailed out of the boat. We were paddling very big water. There is a video of me surfacing and looking at the two ends of my paddle with a puzzled expression. I tried to get hold of my boat and pull it to the side but the water was too big to swim in effectively. I knew that at the end of the run was a very nasty Class V rapid and I didn't want my boat to go down it alone. Eventually I let it go. However much I wanted to save it, I was less keen to swim the rapid myself. Even without the boat the swim to the side was nasty. I took some serious downtime in the waves.

Carl had been on the side filming me. He dropped his camera and ran to join the rescue attempt. Everyone knew that the consequences of a swim on this rapid were serious. I reached the bank and they got me out but my boat went on without me, slid over the last fall and, within seconds the front end was smashed to pieces. Fortunately it was Bala Zapados, my practice boat. I had elected to compete here using her because of the risk in running the last section; her stability should have given me a small advantage. It was a serious loss. Apart from the fact that we had spent hours paddling together and I loved her, Wild Water Racing isn't an Olympic sport and therefore attracts very little funding. Boats of this standard cost about £2,000, a lot of money for a post graduate student to find.

The next day I paddled Lugar Feliz, my happy place. I lost a lot of confidence, though. There were two factors that were now stopping me from competing at my best. I had one paddle left, and was worried that it might happen again; as importantly, I had only prepared myself mentally for the World Championships. Competing at an international level is very tiring, both physically and mentally, and I was starting to feel the strain. I remember talking to Alan Tordoff, our coach about it: he was just happy that I had got back onto the water. Another of the squad, Richard Forbes, had also taken a swim. He had made an error in his paddling and swum down over the fall at the end. To the best of my knowledge he never paddled moving water again. It was a real shame and a loss to the sport.

I had additional help in that Carl, as ever, had my back.

He helped me sort out my other boat and a paddle. My confidence had taken a severe knock. I was battered and bruised and no longer had faith in my equipment, but I knew if I didn't get back on I might never do it again. I took another swim, much further up the course, on the morning of day three so Carl jumped into another boat and joined me. He led me through a couple of runs, stopping just above the nasty rapid. That afternoon we sat above it for a pep talk.

"Look, Gilly, all you have to do is get on and try to get down it. No-one was expecting you to get back on. You've already exceeded everyone's expectation. You aren't doing it for them. Get on and do it for you. Paddle it the way you paddle your plastic boat and enjoy it. You're a good paddler; you've got the skill set. I will be at the start of that rapid waiting for you. I'll make sure you won't go down that last drop."

He had never let me down before and it gave me the confidence I needed.

On the race day a lot of people had dropped out because of the losses of kit and injuries. I wasn't the only person, and we weren't the only team to have lost boats in that rapid. A lot of the female paddlers had withdrawn, everyone was nervous. I was nervous too, but I was also determined to do it. When I reached the end rapid Carl wasn't the only one waiting for me. Alan Tordoff and the other coaches were there to, they ran alongside me, encouraging me all the way. At the end of the run I knew I had beaten it. Carl and the others grabbed my boat and calmed me down again. Winning was a long way from my mind that day. It didn't need to be. I had demonstrated that I had the determination to beat any kind of water. I had also shown some very strong white water swimming skills, for which I received almost as much praise as for my paddling. I had needed them. Alan came to speak to me afterwards. He knew I was targeting being in the top ten in the world, now he was confident that I could do it.

I approached the next three races in Lofer, Austria in a much better frame of mind. It wasn't going to be easy. It had started to rain and just didn't want to stop. The rivers went ballistic. The first race had to be cancelled, which was a shame because in normal conditions it would have really suited me. The next race had to have its course changed because the river was too high to run as originally planned. I was in my element. The high levels really suited me and they also reduced the competition: there were a number of girls who were unhappy paddling at those levels. In practice one of the girls took a nasty swim, panicking as she was carried through large waves, testing the skills of the rescue team. Once again the course finished through a big rapid that was getting bigger all the time. More people dropped out until they shifted the course to give it an easier finish. In each race my paddling improved, building both my experience and my ability.

My Dad brought Mum out to surprise me. They now knew how to handle me at a major competition. Having people there who make demands of you can add a lot of pressure to an athlete which negates the boost that support can provide. Just knowing that they were there gave me a boost and they waited for me to come to them after the race. It was the perfect finish to the series, as they joined the after party, with Dad buying everyone ice cream before we left for home. It was nice to have my parents there to share it with me.

I came back to my PhD but my focus was still on paddling. The selections came through for the Student World Championships which were to be held in September in Kracow. This time I was team manager and they had pulled together a strong squad of eight paddlers, including two that I had trained myself, Kat from Loughborough and Anna, from Bath. It was a very special event for me. This was where I had been scheduled to come in 2002. Which made it a full circle, plus I had a fantastic group of people. Kat was visiting when we got the news; Kat had been selected as non-travelling reserve. This didn't make much sense. If she was good enough to go, why wouldn't she travel? I contacted the BCU who put the selection down to funding. That was another puzzler: the only thing they were funding was our minibus. Kat was devastated so I got back in touch with them and persuaded them that as the trip was mostly self-funded there was no reason for the decision. They relented and I had my dream team ready to go. Kat couldn't quite believe that I had swung it for her, it took an email from the selectors and then a phone call to convince her. She was delighted. She immediately quit her summer job and moved back to Loughborough to train with me.

Our little training squad was back together on the Soar and we worked hard to make sure that we peaked together. The Student World Championships were an amazing experience. We had a road-trip holiday driving out; Pete, my friend from Camp Weequahic came to drive for us, because no-one else had a licence to take a mini-bus and trailer. At the championships themselves many of the world's current most talented paddlers were there. Jon Schofield took gold in the Men's WWR sprint and I came tenth in my race, my highest place in a world event so far. More importantly I had reduced the lead the world champion had over me from 30 seconds to 5 seconds. It was a massive improvement. The whole top ten were very close. We had fantastic team cohesion and, having just been on a World Championship and World Cup tour with them, we knew most of our competitors. After the races we partied right through the night, most of us not going to bed at all. Over the next two days we supported the Slalom team as they competed. The atmosphere was incredible.

Whenever you put serious effort into attaining a goal, there comes a time afterwards when your life seems to be without purpose. It wasn't completely so, but I was exhausted from my summer's competitions. I started writing up my PhD. Although it was an important goal, it didn't have the same excitement that had driven me when I was training for the worlds. Kat came up with a solution.

"You remember when we met, last year?"

"Yes, what about it?"

"You promised to do the Devises to Westminster Race with me."

"You aren't going to hold me to that, are you?"

"Yes. Next year is our year to do it. You told me what your focus was, and you've done your world championships now. This will be the best time for me. I'm a second year and my study schedule works to do it now, so let's go."

"I suppose we'd better, then."

My life became manic again. I had my PhD to write up, I had taken part time work as a lecturer and now I was training full time again. I was back to life the way I like it. For the next eight months I ate, slept, worked and paddled. Kat was almost the only person I saw. We still entered the Wild Water River Races, and fitted in some flat water races, paddling as a pair. It caused a stir. We were two unknowns in Marathon Racing and we were promoted almost immediately up the divisions, beating some very well established crews.

The Devises to Westminster Race is the most demanding event in the British canoeing calendar. From the start in Wiltshire it covers 125 miles with 77 portages. It starts along the Kennet and Avon Canal, before transferring to the River Thames near Reading. Then you have some assistance from the current as far as Richmond. The final seventeen miles are on the difficult Thames tideway. It is raced by most classes in four sections, over four days. Doubles, however, can race non-stop. It means that very careful training and planning are needed, especially to ensure that you get help from an outgoing tide along the tideway. The race always takes place over the Easter weekend, which means there can be some very challenging weather conditions, especially in a year with an early Easter.

The racing world gathered round as it became clear that we would have a chance at putting in the fastest ladies time in many years. John Handyside, the BCU's coaching manager, who had been at the Student World Championships took on the role of our coach. In addition to our tough training schedule we did night paddles and were entered into races to build our experience. Everything seemed to be dropping nicely into place and I couldn't have been happier.

It wasn't to last. In February I was looking at settling down and potentially buying my first house, I had found a great one to look at and wanted to discuss it with my Mum. Tim, Mum's husband called me and I couldn't hold my excitement in about my find, when my heart sunk to find out Mum had been taken into hospital. Tim played it down, I didn't need to go home, but it weighed on my mind. The next day I went to see the house and it was perfect for me. Mum was not kept in hospital so I excitedly phoned home to let her know. She arranged to come up with my sister the next day to see it. She seemed a little restrained, but I put it down to her hospital visit.

My offer to buy the house was immediately accepted, Mum seemed fine. My Mums health has never been the greatest and when she is ill, I feel very vulnerable inside. There is nothing worse than seeing someone you love who is ill and you can do nothing to help them. However, there was nothing I could do and everything seemed to be under control so Kat and I set off with some other students for a Wild Water Race on Dartmoor. I used the tried and tested method I had developed of shelving worries and carried on with life.

The next day was my brother's birthday. I phoned home to wish him a happy birthday but I struggled to get hold of anyone. Finally, I got hold of Tim to find out that Mum was back in hospital with concussion, nothing urgent, no need to come home. After all of the hospital visits of the past week it didn't seem out of the ordinary and we joked about it. I think that was the best way I could think of to deal with the situation.

The next day, after my race, my phone had recorded a lot of missed calls, all from Tim. Signal on Dartmoor is poor and it took me a while to find enough to phone him back. Tim told me that the current diagnosis was that Mum had had a stroke. They weren't completely sure and they were carrying out tests, he would phone me when he knew more. I asked him if he wanted me to come back that evening, but he didn't think it would make much difference.

I was unsettled. As soon as the race finished, we packed my car and loaded our boats and set off for home. I would have to go back to Loughborough to drop Jessica, Jenny and Kat off and I wanted to get started incase I needed to get to Essex. Kat volunteered to drive and Tim called me again once we were on the road. He came through on the hands free.

"It's not good, your Mum's deteriorating." I took it off speakerphone, feeling my insides tense up.

"Do you want me to come home?"

"Not yet but be prepared to"

I felt stuck between a rock and a hard place, we were still driving back from Devon and had just reached Exeter. The whole car had heard the first part of the conversation and there was an awkward silence as we drove along the M5. Nobody spoke for a while and I didn't particularly want to sing to the radio or make light of the situation. We pushed on as fast as we could for home. I was very worried. I was sure Tim wasn't telling me everything. Whatever I decided to do, my first stop was Loughborough. Jenny was staying over for the night which was good. I really didn't want to be alone, and I was unsure if my housemate Rob was going to be home. We had only been back 30 minutes and I had started hanging up my wet kit when the phone rang again. Things had become worse, Tim was not sure if my mum would survive the night and wanted to make sure I had a chance to say Goodbye.

I went about unpacking to repack but my brain was working overtime and I couldn't think what to pack. Rather than keep my fears in, for the first time I called a friend for help and guidance, I phoned Kat who was already in bed and as I garbled nonsense at her, she told me what to pack, primarily not to forget underwear and my toothbrush. I packed a bag quickly. Rob took the boats off my car and promised to look after Jenny. I was in the car and on the road within ten minutes. My family needed me to be strong again, and to look after them, but I wasn't sure I could do it. As I drove through the night I composed myself for what might lie ahead.

I got to the family home in Essex at about two in the morning. My mum had stabilised a bit. It was a very stressful night. Tim headed back to the hospital in the early hours of the morning, after he left, I went and peered in on my sleeping younger brother and checked my sister who also seemed to be sleeping. I sat up with Sally, our family dog and tried to collect my thoughts. It is easy to take the people who are most important to you for granted. When something happens to those people it shakes the foundation of your whole world. Time seemed to be moving slowly. It added a surreal element to the calm around the house.

When the morning came we had to create a semblance of normality; my brother went off to school; I kept my sister company. I put a calm face on a paralyzing inner turmoil. I had been neglecting my family to focus on my PhD and training and in one day one of the most important people in it could have been lost to me. I was panicking and terrified, but I had to show strength for Claire, Josh and Tim. Later that day I visited Mum in hospital. As I lay next to her whilst she tried to formulate words I had a horrible idea of what visiting me in Albuquerque must have been like. I tried to cover it by turning communication into a game. It was almost like playing Pictionary and Charades working out what Mum was trying to say and attempting to finish the sentences together for her. She asked me to look after Claire and to make sure my brother was not scared. I was in awe of my mum. She showed such strength and yet her position was a frustrating one.

Even when things settled down and I was able to come home, I continued to be worried. I was constantly up and down the motorway to Essex and struggling to fit everything in: buying my first house; finishing my PhD; training. I went to see my PhD supervisor and had a heart to heart. I broke down in the meeting and he immediately gave me a month off. Kat and my other friends were marvellous. They supported me and looked after me whenever I was home. They gave unstintingly. On one occasion Kat and I drove to Nottingham for an evening race, but I just couldn't do it. We spent the time sitting in the car park talking before we drove home. I felt much better for it. Slowly Mum improved, but it took its toll on me. I was emotionally drained, but had no real time to let myself recover. I think of that period in my life, as being like a racing car going at full speed.

About a month later everything came to a head, all in one weekend. I had to sit a Viva, the final stage of my PhD. It was the culmination of three and a half years of work. I knew my stuff, I had prepared well, but I was a little blasé about the process. I was given an oral examination by two assessors that took six exhausting hours on the Friday. Afterwards I jumped into a car for the Wild Water Racing selections in Yorkshire. That Saturday was not one of my best paddling days. My brain was fried, but it was more than that. I sat on the start line of the race wondering what on earth I was doing there. I had been training for an ultra endurance event so how could I expect to perform well in a nine minute Classic or a two minute Sprint event as well? It was never going to happen. For the Sunday we crossed the country again, going south to Wiltshire for our last long race before the Devises to Westminster Race. It was a whirlwind, horrid weekend.

Unsurprisingly I didn't get selected for the Wild Water Racing Team. I didn't mind too much. My objectives for my twenty fifth year had been to finish my PhD and win the Devises to Westminster Race. I had completed one of the two and I knew we were in good shape for the second. In the preparation races we had been faster than any other university or ladies crew. A lot can happen in a long endurance event, nothing was certain, but everything was looking positive. Kat was ready for it to.

It's an event that needs a lot of organisation and a big support crew. We would have to take on food and water along the way. John Handyside led four teams made up of students from Loughborough, members of Kat's family and friends. Three teams were tasked with feeding us and the last was to keep our paddling technique on track throughout the event. Kat's family live in Devises which meant that we had somewhere to stay. On the day before we started we took a walk along the canal to watch the Endeavour paddlers setting out on the four day race. The atmosphere was amazing and we got a very strong feeling for the challenge that we were about to start. I was infected with excitement at the first portage and really wanted to start right away, but we had to wait. Non-stop competitors start later and we had a very nervous evening still to go. We ate a large carbohydrate stuffed meal and tried to sleep. Neither of us could so we took Kat's dog for a walk to look at the stars and talk. Eventually we managed a little rest, but there was more waiting to be done the next day. Our start time was 2pm, and we spent the day filling ourselves with food. I was ready to burst long before it was time to go down to the Canal.

As we sat on the line, ready to go, I knew exactly why I was there and exactly what we had to do. For the next twenty hours my only view was going to be Kat's back. Kat has a lot of friends and family in the area who, together with our support crew, gave us a tremendous send off. They made an awful lot of noise. It felt strange to be setting off sedately in such circumstances, but there is absolutely no need to sprint from the line when you have 125 miles to go. We settled into a rhythm and were soon ticking off the miles. It seemed that every bridge had supporters. Every one of them gave us a boost and for a long time our biggest problem was whether we wanted Jelly Babies or Fruit Pastels to chew. It seemed no time at all before we began to portage a lock when a supporter called out to us.

"Well done, only a hundred miles to go!"

"A hundred miles to go," I began to sing, "a hundred miles to go..." Kat joined in. "You take one down, pass it around, 99 miles to go," and we paddled off into the distance singing together. Somewhere that moment has been captured on film.

The light began to fade as we approached Newbury. We had always known that Kat's worst time would be now, as her eyes were adjusting. A low bridge loomed out of the gloom and we had trouble determining whether we could paddle under it or not. It turned out that we could and we soon stopped worrying about such things. Newbury was where the race became more serious for us. We had never paddled further than this before and we were entering unknown territory in terms of our bodies and endurance. We encouraged each other and I helped her to navigate. I had a better memory of what was coming up in terms of bends and bridges.

We arrived at a compulsory stop in Dreadnaught Reach half an hour up on our predicted time. I was receiving regular updates on our progress from our support crew, but this was better than I had expected. I used the information to call on Kat for increases or decreases of speed. We had an opportunity to refuel with hot food and change into dry clothes. We were soon on our way and heading into the darkest part of the night. We were talking less, concentrating on keeping our paddles moving in rhythm and in time. At two in the morning I hit a serious low. Our headlamp went out and we were worrying about getting a time penalty for not having the regulation equipment working. As we approached a portage I reacted badly to being given a progress report. It started with me snapping back and soon degenerated into a shouted argument between, Kat, the crew and me. I lost focus on the task and was trying to put the boat back in the water by myself while Kat was having her light fixed. John pulled us up sharply, reminding us that we were a team and there were two of us in the boat. We felt like two small children and immediately apologised to him. We paddled away in silence for some time before airing our grievances. Before we knew it we were laughing at each other. Kat's new light was working well but a river mist came down and suddenly we couldn't see anything. We saw the funny side of it immediately and by the time we reached the next portage it was if the argument had never happened.

When the sun came up we were both white with tiredness. We paddled on along the Thames until we reached the last portage. There were only eighteen miles to go but we took longer at this point than at any before. My wrists were painfully locked into a paddling position and I was unable to move them. Kat needed cramp tablets. It took a lot of encouragement to get us back onto the water. The tide was with us as we set off on our last section. With only seven miles to go we both hit the wall. We had run completely out of energy and were stopping other crews to try to borrow food. At Putney John, his wife and Anna were waiting for us and we ate everything that they had with them. We had five miles left, but neither of us really wanted to continue. Eventually I paddled us out into the tideway and we had no option. Forty minutes of paddling and it would all be over. I have never in my life been as tired as I was that morning. Kat suffered particularly badly from our sugar low and had spots before her eyes. She concentrated on steering while I paddled.

We began to run into wash from the pleasure boats as we got nearer to Westminster. We saw several other boats capsized by it and didn't want to take any chances. Every stroke I put in I finished with a short support to keep us stable. Eventually Westminster Bridge appeared and we made it across the line. A big cheer went up but we couldn't relax yet. We carefully turned around and made our way to the steps where we clung on to the other finisher's boats. We were just delighted to have finally finished. It was a great feeling. When it came to our turn to get out Kat seemed to leap from the boat. I needed help, but we hugged and helped each other up the steps. We were met by our support crew and both families.

We had paddled the best race we possibly could. We were the first ladies double boat home, the first university crew home and we were the second fastest ladies team ever. That record was set in a very wet year when high currents carried the boats along the Thames much faster than usual. We staggered about like two very drunk but happy people. It took a lot more food before we started behaving more normally once more. The next day, my body collapsed. I had achieved every target I had set myself and had no idea what to do next. I hadn't planned anything to follow and, without the drive of new targets, my stressed body began to stop working and my hair began falling out. I had been so focussed on racing that the only friend I had in Loughborough was Kat. Even my housemate, Rob was constantly away working.

I needed new goals. I took some time to reflect and set my heart on the 2008 Wild Water Racing World Championships. I could happily miss the current year. I love white water more than any other and knew that with the experience of Devises to Westminster behind me I would be able to excel the next year. Kat, Jenny and I decided that we would take a girly trip to the Alps in our plastic boats. I was going to be the leader and we had an awesome time. We paddled some very big rivers, as a result of which both my confidence in leading and my paddling ability went up a notch. Before this I had always done new rivers with Paul, Carl or Adrian, but there I was with just the girls. I lead new rivers on sight. I found that I could lead people down Class IV rapids with ease. It was quite unique for three girls to go out and paddle big rivers for themselves. We tried to collect as many countries as we could, paddling in Austria, France and Italy.

We finished with the Dora Baltea. It originates on the slopes of Mont Blanc and carries a lot of snow melt. It usually runs at about 20 Cumecs but on this day it was running at about 120. It was the biggest water the other two had ever paddled. It looked like the Spean had done on six pipes when I was there with the Frostbite Tour. I've paddled bigger since then but I have never led anything as big. I felt happy all the way, finding the tongues and routes through major stoppers, getting everyone down safely despite them being at the very limit of their paddling ability. It was a major boost to my confidence and when we came back I was ready for the autumn Wild Water Racing season.

The first races were held on the Dee. The British team had had a good season. Jessica had stepped up to the seniors, won some World Cup medals and the European Bronze. Jenny's sister, Sandra Hyslop, had become the Junior World Champion. The whole team was on the verge of a major breakthrough and I was delighted to be back with them. We met up on the Dee. Jessica and Sandra were on fire and I was in contention with them. In the Sprint Race I was a fraction of a second behind, coming third. It was a bit of a wakeup call for them too, but we began to buzz. Paddling this closely together we had the makings of a world beating Classic Team. In the Classic Race I managed to beat Jessica, finishing second to Sandra. We were all within seconds of each other. It was awesome. John Handyside noted how relaxed I was and told me to keep doing whatever it was I was doing.

I was so keen to keep it going that I planned to go back to the Dee with Kat two weeks later. Word got out and before long many of the others were arranging to join us. It became an impromptu GB team training weekend. I concentrated on my weakness, the sprint. I picked out a long concentrated rapid called The Serpent's Tail and began runs of it. Kat was rebuilding her confidence having dislocated her shoulder in September playboating at Nottingham. Carl was there too, supporting me and looking after Kat. We had another student with us learning how to paddle racing boats.

My session was working. Every run I made was faster than the one before. Half way through the session I was running down through The Serpent's Tail when my paddle caught in a rock. I held on to try to pull it out but the boat began to swing across the flow, pulling me over and I felt my shoulder dislocate again. I knew exactly what had happened. This time I was able to roll up and pushed myself into an eddy on river right, just above the constriction at the end of the rapid. The right hand side of the river there is a cliff face: on the left there are a series of long sloped slabs that force the water across to the right and create the rapid. It would have been easy to get out from the slabs. There is also a road an easy walk away. I was in a much harder place. I had caught up with Kat just before entering the rapid and I shouted to try to get her attention. Carl followed soon after with a student he was supporting. I called out to them as they went by in the hope of letting them know that I had a problem. To my relief they both pulled out at the end of the rapid and I could see them talking.

I was stuck in my eddy, unable to paddle, holding onto the side with one hand and bobbing up and down. I had to keep myself calm to stay in control of my situation. Carl came running up the slabs on the other side of the river.

"Are you all right?"

"My shoulder's gone!" We were shouting to be heard over the roar of the water.

"It can't have!"

"Can you get down the next bit?"

"No!"

Carl ran off again. A few minutes later I saw some heads appear above me on the cliff. They had used their boats to cross the river below the rapid. Kat and one of the students worked their way down the cliff to reach me. I popped my deck and between them they pulled both my boat and me to safety. Once off the water the realisation of what this meant hit me. I had been so close: everything had been falling into place. Only two weeks before I had been paddling at the same pace as proven medal winning athletes and now it was all over. I had known I could play for a medal, and Bang! Dream over. Extracting me from the riverside had more problems. I asked Kat to put my arm back in. One of her friends was a shoulder surgeon and had shown her how to put a dislocated shoulder back in. It was my only chance, so I asked her to try. She couldn't do it. I had too much muscle and it was beginning to contract, holding my shoulder out of place.

With Kat supporting me Carl began to try to steer me up to a steam railway line. My balance went off and, without the use of my arm to support me, it was a bit of struggle to get up the cliff. Memories of falling instantly entered my mind and panic set in. At the top Carl sent the other two back to cross the river and summon help. As he guided me back towards the railway station I had a moment of meltdown and Carl did his best to console me. A car met us at the station and took us back to our base to wait for the ambulance. Once there I became obsessed with my Cag. I insisted my friends help me take it off before the medics cut it off me. It was a painful and difficult exercise, but at least it kept us all occupied while we waited. Until they arrived I was able to stay strong, but as soon as they gave me morphine for the pain I relaxed and released my emotions. I was devastated, certain that my World Championship hopes were over but also my competitive paddling career. I needed to train hard to stay at the level I had reached and the dislocation really wouldn't allow me to do that. At Wrexham Hospital they gave me an anaesthetic and put my shoulder back into place. Carl then had to repeat his mission of collecting me. Neither Kat nor I slept well that night, and the next day, as I provided bank support, Kat dislocated her shoulder again. Fortunately one of the other students was able to push it straight back in for her, but it was the end of her training weekend too. We must have looked a strange sight driving home: Kat steering one handed while I changed gear.

This time I had a lot of pain from my shoulder. Something more was wrong than the previous time. I took medical advice and went for an operation just before Christmas. I spent the first two weeks of the New Year having serious physiotherapy with Gill in Essex before returning to Loughborough to train again. I did everything Gill told me, I readjusted my goals, stepped down from World Championship contention because it was going to be a very rough course and decided to aim for the World Cup Series. I worked very hard with John Handyside to get to selection. I surprised everyone, including myself, by coming third.

I had proved before that I could come back from the injury, but this time it was all a bit too much. Over the next few months I began to lose focus. My new goal wasn't what I really wanted. John was concentrating on his World Cup contenders, providing me with training plans but very little other support. Well before we travelled out to the first World Cup Race in Karlovy Vary I was exhausted. The drive that kept me energised while chasing stretching goals just wasn't there.

I raced well at Karlovy Vary. There were two races in the World Cup Series this year, both on shallow fast rivers, with a complicated rapid at the end. I had prepared well for this kind of racing. Many of my friends amongst the competitors knew I had returned from another dislocation and were amazed that I was able to race at all. I finished outside the top ten, but was 45 seconds faster than the previous time I'd raced there. I was now within a minute of the World Champion's time and I was sure I could do better at the next race in Lofer, Austria. We had a week before the next race so the team was off for a few days of training. The previous year the team had found paddling harder water between races had really helped the team's confidence so we went off to find some in Austria. No competitive athlete likes to be left behind, and I felt it was important to let the coaches see that I was still able to be competitive so I joined them on the water. I had paddled bigger water before, but I hadn't prepared my body for this. I was too tired and it was all too much for my shoulder; it was tiring easily and I began to distrust it. On the first day at Lofer, during a practice run, I felt my shoulder move out of place. It popped back, but I knew I couldn't paddle anymore. I could barely lift my dinner plate that evening. I was devastated and withdrew from the race.

It was the start of a decline. This was the last year I would be eligible for the Student World Championships and I had been selected, but too many things were going wrong with me. I finished last. The training season that had started with such strong paddling was ending in disaster. I had lost my focus while I was recovering from my damaged shoulder and the pleasure I got from racing just wasn't there. I had trained and been focussed on competing for more than two years. It was time for a break. I contacted Sam in Albuquerque and flew over in November for two weeks. It was just what I needed. The two of us now had a strong and deep emotional connection. I spent my days resting and reading and in the evenings we put both our worlds to rights.

I returned to England ready to throw myself back onto the rivers. I joined a squad training weekend on the River Usk in Wales. I felt strong, fast and capable, even though the river was in spate and running very high. I was mentally strong enough to stop when my shoulder grew tired and I felt that I was back on course to make the team for the next year. A few days later I woke up with a stiff neck. I eased off my training, expecting it to go away before long, but it didn't. It began to get worse and I made an appointment with Gill, in Essex. I was struggling with simple tasks like putting light weights back onto racks. Gill was worried. She checked my lower back, but didn't want to touch my neck. She advised me to see a specialist as soon as I could. I didn't want to. Surely it would clear up soon, it always had before, and anyway, it was too late in the day to get to a doctor. I decided to sleep on it. The next day I could barely sit up. My doctor decided it was muscle soreness from exercise and sent me home to rest. Things slowly got worse until one day, just before Christmas, I couldn't get out of bed. It took all my effort just to be able to lift my head off my pillow. I seemed to be partially paralysed but managed to crawl out of bed and make my way down to the lounge where Jenny found me and took me to hospital.

The triage nurse took me straight through to the major trauma wing where I was given a series of tests. I wasn't surprised when they put a spinal collar back on me. They told me that it was just a precaution, but deep down, I knew it was more than that. I was transferred to a ward and told I would be there while they sorted out what was wrong and what was needed. I was back to lying on my back staring up at the ceiling in a hospital ward. To make matters worse it was a few days before Christmas. In true Gilly style, I did not want to worry my family, so I kept the whole thing quiet, telling myself, that I would let them know either after the event or when I knew what the problem was. I didn't want any fuss to be made. The only people who knew I was there were Jenny, who took me, and some of the parents of a group of juniors I was coaching: I had to inform them that I would not be there for the session.

On the ward, I began talking to my neighbour. Like me, years before in America, she had her neck in a brace and a similar injury. After two months in hospital she was still flat on her back and looking forward to walking again, maybe. Life had come back full circle and I was back in hospital, wondering what the future held. One thing I was sure of: I wouldn't be settling for walking, maybe. I would be running again as soon as I could.

# 16 GOING FOR GOLD

They let me out of Hospital on Christmas Eve. The C4 to C6 vertebrae are the ones that usually do the moving when you turn your head. Because those had been fused my body was putting pressure on the vertebrae either side of the fused section and they were deteriorating a little. That was putting pressure on a nerve and causing the problem. I was diagnosed with partial paralysis and a prolapsed disk. I needed to rest. For two months I was in and out of a collar as my body repaired itself. It was a difficult time for me. The impact of paddling rough water was causing the problems. I felt that I had to choose between continuing to chase my dream and living a long and active life. I didn't want to give up on either, nor did I want to believe the fact that my neck put me at a disadvantage to others and left me more vulnerable. I went back to Gill and she did her best to help me with physiotherapy. I couldn't paddle white water at all and it was going to take a lot of work to make my neck strong again. I had to focus on getting myself back to doing long walks and general day to day movements, such as being able to sit without discomfort. In that time I lost a lot of muscle and physical conditioning.

Just as I had before, I hid my collar as much as possible from the world. I felt very self-conscious wearing it and didn't want to stand out. Stopping racing made a massive hole in my life. Training and racing had absorbed me entirely. I found that I no longer had any contact with my friends, everyone was out training or racing and I had lost contact with the friends I had outside of that circle. I needed to do something about it and found that I had the time, but lacked the energy for it. I dealt with my isolation by adopting a rescue dog. Poppy needed a lot of care and love and at that time, so did I. We were able to give it to each other and, over time, it is clear that as I have improved in health and mental fitness, so has she. I also picked up the phone and got back in touch with my old university friends. Sally and Sarah, in particular were delighted to hear from me. As my health improved I began to paddle again, just gently, with Paul.

My neck had caused me to have to rest, and I was desperate to get my fitness back. I knew it wouldn't be easy, and that it would take time. I needed a goal to work towards. I decided that a challenge was needed and I would concentrate on getting walking fit. I called Sam in Albuquerque and arranged to go over for another visit in the summer. I always felt better visiting Kim, Jen and Sam. I wanted to go back to the Grand Canyon and walk all the way down to the Colorado River at the bottom. It was an achievable goal. It was challenging because my health was coming back slowly and the climate in England is very different. In Arizona I would need to be able to cope with altitude, heat and humidity on a very different scale. All the same, I thought that if I put the same planning into this goal as I had done for the world championship and Devises to Westminster Race, I could achieve it. I booked three weeks in America. Sam was busy at the start of my visit, so that would be when I did my walk, but then we would have two lovely long weeks together. I didn't share my other goal with her: I wanted to go back to the Sandia Mountain and climb it by the La Luz Trail. The time felt right but I didn't want to give Sam stress by telling her. It turned out that I didn't need to. She knew what was on my mind and was making plans to help me in her own special way.

The Canyon was just as captivating as I remembered it. The colours were brilliant and changed as the sun reflected on the rocks. I pitched my tent and walked quietly along the rim, lost in the magnificence of it. I felt a deep contentment. I knew that this trip was going to make a big difference to how I felt about myself. I was in bed early and the next day went for a shorter walk to acclimatise. I hiked four miles down a trail and walked slowly back up. My body took the exercise well, I had worked out my pacing for going down and going up the trails, and I knew that I would be fine the next day. I marvelled as the sun set that night and was up before it rose again.

The Bright Angel Trail is very well defined and quite spectacular. Going down it is easy and, having started early, I covered the nine miles to the river in just over two and a half hours. It was still only 7:30 in the morning and I was bouncing around taking pictures. The walk back up was much harder. At the Indian Garden campground, a prominent landmark on the trail, I took some time out to shelter from the sun. I began a conversation with another walker and before long we talked ourselves into a three mile diversion, on the Plateau Point Trail. It added a considerable time to both of our expeditions but it was very worthwhile. We walked together all the rest of the way back to the rim. We had both been walking alone and it was nice to have some company. The co-operation was good for both of us, too: I kept him going and he slowed me down, which meant that I took in much more of the views.

I drove back to Albuquerque the next day and met up with Sam. I couldn't wait to see her and when I appeared at her doorstep it was as if I had only seen her the previous day. I had come so far since she had waved me onto a plane in a wheelchair. It had been a rollercoaster journey, in terms of my physical recovery and mentally I had finally begun to accept what had happened and that I may never have an answer to some of my 'Why' questions.

We set off a couple of days later for a week of camping and walking in Colorado and Utah. I experienced the massive contrasts of climate and terrain that this part of America provides: my first ever sandstorm in Utah and the beautiful forested hills around Aspen. Back in Albuquerque I revealed my plan to Sam. She agreed to come with me and we set off to follow the La Luz Trail. It wasn't as if I had much option. She had always said that if I ever went up there again she would be going with me.

We started in a different place, on the proper trail rather than on a connecting path, and it was very easy to follow. Sam wasn't as fit as I was so we stopped regularly to take in the view and give her a rest. It took a long time to get out of the foothills but eventually we were winding our way up the mountain. I kept getting ahead, so every so often I would stop and wait for her to catch up. At one of these stops, near a marker post, I paused and looked around. There was an option here to go left to a little cabin or on and up to the Tram. I turned around to take in the view and felt a shock go through me. There was a hump of rock just off the trail that I recognised as the top of the boulders where I had begged Mike to take me back down off the mountain. It was the highest point we had reached and it was right beside the trail.

I perched on a rock to take it in more clearly. I could see where we had walked anticlockwise around the top of it; I could see the ledge that I had hopped down onto before setting off down the gully that had led to the cliff; I could see where the bushes obscured the view of our way back to the actual trail.

I was in absolute turmoil. For a moment I thought I might cry, but my tears didn't quite come. My mind was racing, remembering the state that I was in when we reached that point, trying to work out how we had failed to see the path. I debated pushing through the bushes to see why we had missed it. It might not be clear from there, but I didn't want to tempt fate by standing on it. I considered hiding my discovery from Sam. I have never been happy showing my feelings and for a short while I turned my back on it, getting ready to lead off when she arrived. But if there is one person in the world I can always share my feelings with, it is Sam. Quite often I don't even need to say anything. She can read me like a book. As she approached me I turned back to her and pointed.

"This is it. This is where we got to before turning around!"

Sam put her arms around me. I didn't need to explain anything more, she could put all of the pieces of the jigsaw together herself, but I needed to explain for my own sanity. Like a true friend, she just listened and made no judgments of me. I pointed the details of the place out to her. The emotion was too much for me. I pulled out of her arms and ran a little way up the trail to try to sort out my emotions. The memories of walking around that point were so clear that it was as if I was still there, they had so much colour, taste and feel to them. Sam sat down and waited, patiently. After a little while, when the memories began to move back into the past, I made my way back to her. We were both quite shaken and made our way slowly up towards the top. It was important for both of us to have found the place, and I only saw it by chance. As we went on the trail twisted above the gully. By going to the edge I could identify more places, including the small ledges that had finally been my undoing and possibly even the place I had lain and waited for rescue. The ridge I had been able to see above me that night was where I was now standing. All of the pain, fear and worries of that night on the mountain came back to me and then, as if by magic they slowly began to fade away. I pressed on to the top and stood tall, raising my arms to the sky. I had done it: seven years after setting out I had walked to the top of the Sandia Mountain.

My hands moved to touch my hair and the back of my head and I had a good stretch pushing my elbows out to the side. I stood tall and took in a deep breath. I looked at the sky once more, as I breathed out, and with the breath all my shelved emotions, memories and angst were released into the sky. I was freed from them at least. I couldn't pin down which ones, other than I now felt lighter and I no longer had a driving need to reach the top of the mountain. I was free.

We had planned that I would walk back down, but that Sam would take the Tram. Just getting up the mountain was more exercise than she was used to taking. Looking at me, Sam didn't want to leave me alone. She told me that she hadn't brought any ticket money with her; she wanted to walk. I was surprised. I had enough money with me to buy her ticket, but it was clear that she wanted to stay with me to give me support. I decided to say nothing about it and accepted her offer. The company was what I needed, and Sam knew that without being asked. It later turned out that she did have the money. The journey down was difficult, it rained once again and Sam was struggling with tiredness. We supported each other down on a very emotional journey. I took her and Jen out that evening for a meal to celebrate. Without Sam, Jen and Kim I don't know how I would have got through the trauma of my fall. Whenever my recovery became difficult I would call them and talk to them. They had visited me in England and I had gone back several times to spend time with them in Albuquerque. Every single time, however hard the parting, I had come away stronger and with more belief in myself. When I first went to America I felt that I had the space to become myself properly, something which my fall had taken away from me. Somehow Sam, in particular, was able to put me back in touch with that Gilly, the girl who could do anything and at long last I finally had the chance to give her something back. Her long term boyfriend, Chris Vigil, had trouble expressing how he felt and their relationship was in trouble. I could see how much they loved each other and Sam had told me how she felt. I had an opportunity to talk to him and suggested that Sam needed to know he cared as much for her as she did for him. It was nice to be a listener for a change, rather than the one speaking.

The next morning I flew out again, back to the UK. We had our usual tearful parting but for the first time I didn't need to hang onto my last view of the mountain. The feeling stayed with me. I was a professional coach at the time, developing juniors in Canoe Sprint and Canoe Slalom to international level. At one of the National Regattas everyone seemed to notice the difference. I was happier and much more relaxed. I had relived the day on the mountain every single year on its anniversary and for the first time I didn't. I had a normal day. I have never had to go through it again.

A week after I came home from the States I had an email from Sam demanding that I call her immediately.

"You have to come back out."

"You what? Why?"

"You are going to be my bridesmaid, aren't you?"

"Of course I'll come back to the States!"

"I'm going to tell you off when you get here."

"Why? What have I done now?"

"You didn't tell me you had a word with Chris. You made him ask me."

"No, I didn't. He wanted to ask you; I just helped him find the words."

In the Spring I went back to the States to be Sam's bridesmaid. It was a wonderful experience. I still feel I have another family there. I knew most of the people in the room: her whole family, her friends and even most of their friends. I haven't needed to go back since, but I know I haven't been to Albuquerque for the last time.

My health improved steadily. I was building up slowly, being careful: my plan was to be back in a racing boat the following year so in November I went for a long weekend on the Dart with my friends Adrian and Carl. It was a recreational trip, paddling plastic boats and in the same format as my first visit, so many years ago; the difference being that I paddled with them as a coach. Shortly after I came back I began to feel ill. There were a number of viruses going around and I put it down to a bad bug. I was weak and feverish. These symptoms were the same as my friends were having. Body spasms and lack of co-ordination weren't, but I wasn't ready to admit to having them. I spent a week in bed and got up again feeling slow and without energy. I was recovering, though, so I didn't go to the doctors or tell anyone about it. I just went doggedly back to my life.

In the January it struck again. I had a new job, working for Sports Coach UK on building modern coaching programmes for a range of sports. I was in a meeting in Loughborough when I began to feel ill. I had nausea and the shakes. I tried to cover it up but it was too much and eventually I had to excuse myself and go home. The lack of coordination symptoms came back, together with a weakness in the right side of body. My first port of call was my physio, Gill. She has helped me back to fitness and I know that she understands me. I was relying on her magic touch. My biggest fear was that my neck repair was breaking down. If it did I was convinced that I wouldn't be as lucky as I was the first time, and even if I was how could I find the strength to go through such a long recovery again? Gill reassured me that my neck was fine, but then she told me in no uncertain terms that there was something wrong and I needed to go to see the doctor.

I reluctantly made an appointment. My doctor was puzzled and brought the other doctors from the practice in to the consultation as they tried to work out was going on, with comparative strength and coordination tests on both sides of my body. Eventually they referred me for blood tests and a visit to a specialist. Now I was really worried. I know that my nervous system is weak. It is a residual effect from the spinal damage I had sustained on the Sandia Mountain. I had been hiding from being unwell; the longer I took no action, the longer I could pretend that nothing was really wrong and that I would recover as I always have done. Injured Gilly isn't really me. She is a character I watch from a distance because I can't cope with the concept of not being at my best all the time.

I was scared. I was determined not to wait and paid for a private consultation. I went for brain scans the very next day. Looking at her screen the technician told me that she expected me to need to come back for scans from more angles. I took this as an indication that she could see something unexpected and spent the week it took for them to come through worrying about my future. When I finally saw the specialist it was clear that there was something wrong.

"This area of your brain is completely normal, but this here is abnormal," he said, pointing out a series of pea shaped shadows across my brain. "They are very like the lesions we would see with Multiple Sclerosis, but they are still rather small and not clumped in the way that MS lesions are. They are unlikely to be tumours but we need to investigate them fully and take some samples of brain fluid for analysis." I didn't really take anything else in. After all I had been through I now had a brain problem. Once again I had gone to the appointments on my own and not told people I had a problem. I was fearful of showing my weaknesses or vulnerability. Even though deep down I did not want to be on my own, I did not have the confidence to ask for help from my friends. There was only one thing I could do: I went back into denial and straight back to work. Even though I did my best to hide, word had spread that I wasn't well and my colleagues, both new and old friends like Kat, treated me very well.

The time had come to tell my family and Claire came with me to get the results from the Lumbar Puncture. They were inconclusive. This was both good and bad news: with a diagnosis you can start treatment, but if they can't diagnose it then perhaps it isn't so serious. Eventually a decision was reached that I had some symptoms of Multiple Sclerosis and some neuro-muscular degeneration which is a side effect of my spinal injury. I could deal with that.

I began a slow recovery program of physiotherapy and exercise. As a woman of action, I changed my job to lighten my work load, moving to Lincoln University to lecture in Elite Sports Performance and Biomechanics. Even though I loved the type of work I was doing the driving was making me tired. The tiredness seemed to enhance some of the symptoms I was experiencing which in return meant I could not undertake some of the core things I loved about life: paddling on white water and generally being out in a boat.

I hadn't planned to go back to academia but it was a much lighter physical workload and I needed that. As I settled into work, I began getting my physical fitness back into shape. I was much better than I had been but I had very little endurance. I found after twenty to thirty minutes of exercise my body would start to fail. I would lose co-ordination or start to shake and my strength would go on one side. I hadn't let go of my dream, if anything it burned even more strongly. I wanted my dream: to be the best that I could be; to be on a podium; to be the best in the world. I began to rethink. I studied long and hard, consulted anyone I thought could help and found new ways to train, new ways to build up my fitness. It took two years of constant work and adaptation to achieve.

In 2011 I went for River Racing selection again. I wrote my own training programs. Anything over twenty minutes was out but, with the help of my new academic friends, people within canoeing and Gill, I worked out how to do most things within that time. Gill soon felt that my condition and strength was better than it had been for a long time. The longest I had been able to work was thirty five minutes. Carl helped me out enormously. He was there for me on the rivers, he drove me to them, so I could optimise my time on the water, as my short time window often applied to driving as well.

We found a way for me to have a break between sessions and things began to come together. The selection event took place on the Tryweryn, my favourite river. Sandra and Jessica were still the top paddlers and they had been joined by Hannah Brown. The three of them had picked up the Gold Medal in the Classic Team Race the year before and they had a pile of other medals between them. They were the girls to chase.

My Classic Race went well and I knew I was in contention. My first Sprint run went well, too, I was right on the pace I needed. I felt strong and was completely confident as I went all out for it. The graveyard is a technical Class IV rapid that needs every paddle stroke to go in the right place for a successful run in a racing boat. Halfway down, in a chicane style manoeuvre, I slightly mistimed a stroke. My boat went off the line, throwing me over into a half roll before spinning out of the flow into a micro-eddy. I broke back out again in a manoeuvre more typical of a plastic river boat. I lost around nine seconds and was six seconds down on Hannah's time. I was very disappointed: I was sure I would have been close to her, but for that slip. The whole event was scored on a points system and I wasn't selected.

It's difficult to be objective when you want something that much. At times I felt that I had missed my place on a technicality, at others I understood that, even though I couldn't have put any more into that second Sprint run, on the day things just hadn't gone my way. I managed to become objective and for the second time ever I was content that I couldn't have done anymore. For the first time I was pleased with what I had achieved. I didn't have to prove anything to anyone and that included me. It was a huge milestone for me. I was also left without a focus for the rest of year when Dee Paterson, my team-mate at the Karlovy Vary World Championships in 2006 called me.

"Come and do Dragon Boat Selection."

"Dee, I've never been in a Dragon Boat."

"Doesn't matter. Just come and do the selection race. It'll be a giggle."

"What do you race in?"

"An Oh-One"

"What's one of those?"

"It's like a flat-water boat but you paddle with a toothpick. Come down and borrow a boat. It's only five hundred metres. Just have a go. You'll be fine."

It was great to see her at the selections, but she was the only person I knew there. There were lots of people lining up and looking nervous but I didn't really feel it. The canal we would be racing on was nothing like as fearsome as the Tryweryn. Someone brought me a boat and some long, strange looking poles over.

"Dee asked me to lend you this. Do you know how to put it together?"

"I've got no idea what to do with it."

"Someone else is going to lend you a paddle."

"OK." She helped me put it together. It looked like a fairly stable flat-water racing boat with an outrigger. I jumped in.

"Dee, what do I do?"

"Put the blade in the water and pull, Gilly." It was a single, narrow bladed paddle that you used in a similar way to a C1 boat or an open canoe.

"Aren't you supposed to push? Push it down?"

"Don't you get all technical with me." We were gathering looks. Dee was clearly well known and people were starting to want to know who she was bantering with. I had a quick practice and Dee told me that I had more or less got it. Before long it was time for my trial run. My first run was the first time I tried to paddle it at speed. I recorded the second fastest time of the day. They wanted me to try paddling on my opposite side. I applied what I had learned in the first run and knocked a couple of seconds off my previous time.

I met up with Carl later that evening and tried to explain my experience to him. Compared to everything I had done before it seemed a very bizarre kind of paddling. Before the end of the evening I heard that I had been selected. Sadly I had knocked Dee out of the boat. It took me a few minutes to decide whether to accept. I wanted the opportunity, but felt very bad about taking my friend's place in the crew. It didn't take long to work out that, as a competitive paddler, Dee would happily take someone else's place and that I should too. I accepted.

There were training weekends pretty much every other week. I was worried about the effort involved, but was reassured that sessions would generally be within my thirty minute threshold. It was a team event, you share the boat with nineteen other paddlers, a drummer and a helm. The sport is still young: the first World Championship was held in 1995, but it has rapidly spread across the world. As soon as I got into a crew boat I began to love it. At the first training weekend I quickly realised that the level of organisation had not yet reached the levels of more established sports. I offered to help and began writing training schedules for my team mates.

We flew out to Tampa in Florida in July 2011 and came away with Bronze Medals for both the Open and the Mixed boats. It was a big moment for me. I was paddling in both boats so I finally stood on a podium and received not one, but two World Medals. The fact that I stood there with a whole crew of others meant little at the time. I had never worked in such a close team before and I loved every minute of it.

Just before the final celebrations of the championship, I sat in my room and stared at these two medals in my hands. They didn't feel real, even though I had won them. In a Dragon Boat, there are 20 people in the boat. Team work is vital: if one person tries to put more effort in than the others, it can actually be detrimental and slow the whole boat down throwing off the timing and pacing of the stroke of those sat around you. For me, with so many people to share the experience with, my individual input felt a little lost. Deep down I still longed for individual glory where I was in charge of my own boat. These medals in front of me were not to be belittled. In the world's total population, how many sit on a start line of a World Championship and then what percentage actually win medals? Not many. I was very privileged to have such an opportunity! I needed to remember that and not dismiss the achievement, as well as the journey I had taken to get there.

On our return I was asked to help some more with the team's training. We were out to win better medals at the European Championships the next year. I set up a training camp and we looked at every member's performance individually, writing them personalised training plans. I had bigger ideas than that. I wanted to professionalise the whole process but my body was becoming unreliable again. My back went into spasm in October. I was in constant pain and had to take ten weeks off from work and training. I lost a lot of weight and my fitness plummeted once more. I took solace in the thought that I could at least go to the Championship as the team coach.

This problem affected my thinking as well as my health. I was still working as a lecturer in elite sports performance and also as a coach to some elite athletes. If I couldn't be fit at that level and hadn't achieved my individual goals, how could I advise and train others to get there? Could I even be around them? I had unfinished business, I had so much more to give and achieve, but if my back wasn't going to get better I needed a challenge which wasn't focused solely around sport and athletes. I thought that having such an active job would not help my body in recovering so I slowly came to the idea that perhaps I needed a desk job. This was something I never ever saw myself having, I was quite free spirited, loved being outdoors and had never been in an office environment. However, if I was to have any chance in achieving my dreams, I needed to do what was best for my body. If there was a slim chance I could continue competing, I had to find a way to do it, I would rest whilst at work. I began searching for different industries that I could use my skill set in. After some enquires, I had secured an interview in a completely different field of work from sports, I quit my job and after a break, went to work for a Car Manufacturer using the maths method from my PhD.

As I began to recover I was able to work on my fitness again. I began to train lightly in March 2012. Four weeks later I was able to enter selection for the GB Dragon Boat team. At selection I was one of the fastest paddlers in the squad. I was still the strength and conditioning coach for the team and I began working more closely with the ladies team and I worked hard with them over the next few months. We set out to become elite athletes, changing and intensifying the way we all worked. It paid off. When it came to the championships I was proud to stand beside them, to climb into the boat and to paddle with them. I was paddling in two crews. With the Ladies team we won two Gold Medals and a Silver one. In the Mixed team we swept the board in every distance, taking three Gold Medals. It was the peak of my athletic career, both as a coach and as a paddler.

It wasn't my original dream, it was a different one. It was still the moment that I had dreamed of. Sometimes when life throws you challenges you have to adapt your dreams. In climbing onto the podium with the team I had achieved so much more than I could ever have done on my own, I had made the dream come true, not just for me but for every one standing there with me. The medal I am proudest of is not one of the Gold medals that I was given there, but the one the team presented me with, in the bar afterwards, for coaching them. I will treasure it forever.

# 17 MAKING A NEW FUTURE

Whenever I achieve my goals I find myself wondering what to do next. It leaves a hole in my life which needs filling. Winning the European Dragon Boat Gold medals was an amazing experience. It fulfilled some important ambitions for me but it has also left me wanting more. I have taken some time out to reflect, to write this book and decide what to do next.

Looking back on how you learn to paddle white water and the lessons it teaches you, I realise they have been useful throughout my entire life without me even realising it. I believe they are ones that anyone can use. To paddle white water well, to get to the bottom of a rapid, upright, in control and having enjoyed the experience can be one of the best moments in your life. The lasting memories can be both good and bad and but if you are clever you can change a bad experience into a good one. Just as falling off a mountain for me became of the best things to have ever happened to me.

The first lesson I learnt was to know where you want to get to; to focus your attention on where you want to go in front of you, rather than where you have been or where you are currently. For many people, their anxiety only allows them to look at the front of the boat and they do not have the confidence or courage to tilt their head up and look ahead of them. They are stuck either in the past or in the present and no further. They react to the moment rather than try to pick a route forward. As Paul puts it: "What is their plan?" Often in white water, this can lead to someone swimming because the water they are looking at in front of them is where they will end up. Whenever, I have a plan, I know that there is no hole to cover up or be swallowed up into. As I make each stroke, my confidence increases and so does the pace at which I do it.

The second is that actually getting to where you wish to go comes from a combination of experiences. In my white water analogy: different types of strokes and how you use them. Every time, forward strokes are the best strokes, but often I have wished to put a back stroke in or a sideways one, when the world is going too fast for me to keep up with. When I put a back stroke in, I am allowing the water to begin to take control of the boat rather than me be in control of the water. A back stroke slows the speed of the boat down at the cost of control. So now I try to put a forward stroke in and just slow it down, it has the same effect as a backstroke as it acts a bit like a brake but gives me time to look, compose and make my decision for my next stroke. I can combine my forward slowed stroke with a bit of a side movement which helps me steer to where I wish to be. This might be a different route altogether.

When paddling down a rapid, there are often many different routes or paths. As a beginner, you find it hard to see any paths, but when you open your eyes and you seek out the knowledge of others around you, you begin to see what you could do. Then when you decide to attempt a specific path, you start to see options: perhaps the left or right looks more fun or is easier or, equally, it looks harder and you want the challenge. For me, paddling down a rapid is like my life, you begin on one path and a wave can unexpectedly take you on another. You just need to keep paddling with a forward stroke.

The final most useful lesson is that you cannot achieve it alone. I have tried far too many times and failed. I can get stuck on one manoeuvre and my life starts t resemble the film 'Groundhog Day', and no matter how many times I try to run it, I am stuck. I could miss it and pretend but it comes back to haunt me, it becomes a bigger and bigger nemesis. In my past no one could fault me on the effort I have put in to try and achieve goals. I have missed so many and shelved the emotional defeat. It is only when I am forced to admit I need help that I am overwhelmed with people who are there to support me. I have found mentors or friends who have a method to attack it with; or those who will jump on and sit next to you and try it with you and help you find that smile.

Writing the book has helped me to put much of my past into context. I have been able to see all of the hidden jigsaw pieces of the mountain adventure and for most of them it is the first time I have been able to attach the emotion associated with it. I cried for the first time when retelling the events of the night when I made the decision to give up on life. To admit, openly, how scared I was on so many occasions where previously I have I tried to disguise it with humour as I quickly put on my armour to protect my soft inner core. I seldom take time to appreciate what I have actually achieved and the circumstances I have had to do it. For me, personally, many of my achievements feel like normal everyday occurrences that people have to overcome, a bit like getting out of bed each day. As I am the one living it, it is the norm, but it is not someone else's norm.

When I came back from representing my country, I came back to everyone else's normal routine of getting up and going to work. Sitting on start lines or nervously sitting in a changing room feels like a distant memory.

However, when I have been coming back from an injury or a physical set back it feels like I am climbing mountains just in order to complete everyday tasks and just getting through a 'normal day' is like completing an ultra marathon. So I go from one end of the scale to the other and to ground myself I go back to the advice I was give by Kat for the start line of the world champs, which was to pause and smile.

I have not openly gone about celebrating my past achievements: in reality my greatest was coming back to live another day after falling. I was far too embarrassed at my own stupidity. Over time I have admitted to myself I made a mistake that day. I was more worried about what people would think of me, that they would all think I was stupid and had 'Failure' written all over my face; that they wouldn't want to have anything to do with me. I thought I had failed my family, my friends and most of all I had failed myself. From the day it happened until quite recently, I have tried to dumb down what occurred and most of all that night. I have tried to reduce the scale of the task I had in recovering and how the impact of the event is sculpting my future.

In reality, it is unlikely I shall ever be able to do another attempt at Devizes to Westminster race, due to the way the fall affects my central nervous system and the amount of exercise my body can handle in one period of time. However, I will never say it is impossible as I love to attempt impossible tasks. The disks between my vertebrae may be degenerating and the movement I once had in my neck is now on a decline so I suffer more frequently from muscle spasms. It could be seen as a negative, but it is the reality. My degradation in my cognitive movements, is something I need to manage and when required change my lifestyle to adapt, so I can continue doing what I love doing. It is yet another problem I need to find alternative solutions for. I just need to remember to keep talking, search for new ideas, let people around me support me and not be quite so stubborn in my attempts to do it all on my own. The biggest hurdle I have to overcome is actually letting people into and under my armour.

Reflection is one of my most important tools. I have a habit of focussing on the physical and neglecting the mental. I have learned the hard way that each is half of the whole and unless they are both in peak condition I will never perform as well as I might. It is always easy to measure your physical fitness. You can perform tests and see the results. Mental preparation is harder to see, but if it is neglected it can derail the physical machine in an instant. After my fall I was totally focussed on getting back on my feet and chasing my physical goals. Neglecting my mental recovery caused me to come close to break down and slowed my recovery. With hindsight I am sure I would have recovered to full fitness more quickly if I had taken up the offer of rehab. I didn't take it for the wrong reasons: I associated it with being ill and my state of denial said that I was no more than inconvenienced by my fall; I had things to prove. Rushing my recovery meant that I had to deal with compensatory injuries from over using the parts of my body that still worked and that I was haunted by my night on the mountain for seven years. I still am, but now I am more comfortable with what happened.

Reflection brings self knowledge. It allows you to learn from your mistakes and to accept that they are essential for your development. After the level of reflection that has gone into producing this book I am in the strongest mental position I have ever been in. It is allowing me to review my future goals with a greater degree of clarity and I know that when I set them they will be right for me. I have two constant voices in my head. They can be represented by my two friends, Paul and Carl.

Paul is the voice urging me on: "Come on Gilly, it'll be fun and you know you can do it: a top ten World ranking. You have unfinished business."

Carl is more measured: "Why do you want to do it?

What are you trying to prove and who to? You have nothing to prove!"

I have learned the hard way that it is fine to be afraid and to show my weaknesses to others. In fact sometimes we need to embrace it. This could be what I did when I let go of the root. I am still haunted by the fear of feeling alone and that fear is intertwined with my inability to stop. I battle with it daily. Over time I have found ways to manage it but I have not yet found the best one. The fear of loneliness began during my school years and it escalated in the quiet and darkness of the mountain. When I was looking up at the ridge I longed for my friends and family to be with me. I didn't want to die alone; I think that was a significant driver of my stubbornness through that long night and is, perhaps, the thing that brought me back to life.

The loneliness hits me most when I allow self doubt to creep up on me, often when I know I am returning to my house, and I will be on my own. It is the quietness I dread and the associated darkness that sends me into a panic. It clouds my thoughts and I struggle to see any future beyond it. In the early years after the fall, I could be consumed by my fear. I would go into myself and sometimes it could take days or weeks for me to bring myself out of it. My self-protection would not allow me to admit or communicate my weakness to others so I would avoid the problem and keep busy. However, your body is a clever thing: it shows your unhappiness in many other ways. Blank looks, inability to find words and a manic need to just keep going were a few of mine.

You do have to face your problems eventually. Avoiding them only means that you have to do it when you hit rock bottom. This happened to me when I dislocated my shoulder and I realised I couldn't be strong Gilly any longer. I went to Carl to talk it through with him and try to rationalise it. This was the first time I had ever been able to open up to another person in my life. My inability to stop was driven by my worry that if I did so, my body would also stop. I had given up on life once and the shame of it engulfed me: I have promised myself I will never do that again. My body will stop only when it is ready to.

I have been afraid of admitting to fear, which seems to me to be the silliest kind of fear there is. I have learned over time that when that panic and darkness comes over me I need to call a friend or make a plan so I have something to look forward to. My closest friends can see this panic rise in me: I often find myself visiting and staying with them while they provide me with that helping hand. I am still learning how to deal with my fears and over the year it has taken to write this I have realised and taken on board the reality that if you don't listen and switch off then your body will deteriorate faster. This is something I have to face and deal with. Rest as well as pacing things gives your body a chance to reflect and build upon the effort it has put in. Dealing with these fears and learning from my mistakes has freed me up to put more effort into achieving my goals and directly helped me to success with the Dragon Boat Team.

It is very important not to let conditioning hold you back. We have attitudes and expectations ingrained in us from our earliest childhood. These can be especially restrictive for women. They have a pervasive affect on our thinking that means that even when we are successful we can underestimate what we have done. I have never really believed in my paddling ability. I always compared myself to people who were better, I never really allowed myself to approve of what I had done. Reflection helps us to see how far we have come. It allows us to take away the confidence we need from our achievements and to reach for the next goals. I believe that to truly have self confidence you have to stop seeking the approval of others and take the time to appreciate and approve of yourself.

I have a set of new goals that I'm looking at now, for

the future.

I would like more than anything to achieve my dream of being on the podium in my chosen sport, white water racing. Perhaps 2014 will be my year, as I have been selected for the World Championship and World Cup team, after an absence of 6 years. My mind is in the best possible place and so is my body. So if the two can work in harmony on and after that fifth and final 'boop...' anything is possible if I believe. However, I may get there and find the white water pounds my body too much. I know that I may have to switch my dream that it might not be me on the podium but someone I help, or it might be a different type of podium altogether. That is what makes life exciting.

I've come a long way since the day I let go of a root on the Sandia Mountain and apologised to the world, both out loud and quietly. Before that day I had almost drifted into the things I had achieved, from GCSEs to A-Levels. I can predict that I would have continued this trend and never have known what it is like to really, really want something when it is slipping out of your grasp, and how hard you actually need to apply yourself to getting it back. I lost my childhood assurances as well as deep rooted places in my soul that I unconsciously used to protect myself. I had to build a new life for myself to make the most of my second chance at life. I am proud of what I have achieved. I wanted to run again: In order to do that I had to learn to walk, it was a logical process for me. I often use the analogy of 'If you aim for the stars, you will hopefully reach the moon'. That is what I did and still do. That's why I always try to look up.

# ABOUT THE AUTHOR

My name is Gillian Mara but most know me as Gilly. The 28th August 2002 was a pivotal day in my life and one I shall never forget. It was just before my final year of university: I had decided where I wanted to go with my career and was about to achieve a childhood dream of competing for Great Britain in canoeing. I was a confident, outgoing individual with a real zest for life. The world was my oyster!

I fell approximately 200 feet. In the early stages after the fall, as I began my recovery, I was plagued with unanswered questions, how and why did it happen are just some of them. However one thing was said to me that stuck in my mind; 'You have to want to get better'. I made a very conscious decision there and then that I didn't want to walk again - I wanted to run!

Out of my own sport of Canoeing, I was heavily involved in sport in all aspects. I have coached at world class level, been a national coach educator and been involved in developing coaching qualifications for numerous sports. My ability to think out of the box proved a breath of fresh air to some sports in making people think and then coach in a different way. The skills picked up from completing a doctorate in sports engineering, where I worked alongside sports manufacturer adidas and my experiences as a coach and an athlete led me into lecturing and then finally into working in occupant and vehicle crash analysis at an automotive company as well as an athlete mentor. The journey I have taken since falling has all had the same underlying theme behind it and that is a real need to help others and to make a difference. I take great pleasure in overcoming challenges and solving problems.